P9-DGJ-689

The Problems of Union Power

VOLUME 1, SERIES 1, 1961

BY

JOHN M. COURT

Published and distributed by

Labor Policy Association, Inc.,
1624 Eye Street, N. W.,
Washington 6, D. C.

Price $3.50

TABLE OF CONTENTS

INTRODUCTION

"The Problems of Union Power," by John M. Court of Williamsburg, Virginia, was given the first of the annual awards offered in September 1960 by Labor Policy Association for the best paper submitted on that subject by students, graduate students, and faculty members in certain fields of study during the academic year 1960-1961. Mr. Court was a graduate student of law at the College of William and Mary and is now practicing law at Newport News, Virginia.

This thoughtful study states the problems, analyzes them, examines their components, draws conclusions, and recommends remedies. Although the author's recommendations are firmly grounded in his profound belief in the virtue of our federal system and the capacity of our people to govern themselves, they may be expected to draw fire from an assortment of vested interests, both in and out of government.

The purpose of the awards which led to the writing of this book was to stimulate organized study, constructive thinking, and understanding of one of the most widely discussed and least comprehended domestic issues of our day, the issue encompassed by the term "the problems of union power," often referred to more loosely as "the union monopoly problem."

The directors and members of Labor Policy Association in the past several years have become acutely aware of the need for some first-class minds to give the uninterrupted study required for comprehensive knowledge and understanding of the whole problem of union power. The establishment of the awards was an attempt to encourage qualified scholars and future leaders of thought to seek solutions to the problems involved here; solutions within the framework of our system of limited government, a free market, and a scrupulous regard for the rights of men.

With considerable satisfaction we present this first of a contemplated series of such award-winning studies to be published annually on the subject, "The Problems of Union Power."

WILLIAM INGLES,
President,
Labor Policy Association, Inc.

The whole history of civilization is strewn with creeds and institutions which were invaluable at first, and deadly afterward.

WALTER BAGEHOT: Physics and Politics, 1869

FOREWORD

The navigator at sea is obliged to make a series of assumptions as to his position, course and progress, and then by a series of measurements of various celestial bodies in relation to a visible horizon, and a series of logical deductions therefrom, estimate how far he is from where he thought he should have been. Thereupon he may recommend a new course and speed to reach the port of destination. It is a homely method but it has brought many a ship to port safe from a perilous voyage.

Essentially this pragmatic empirical approach is the one used here in the field of industrial relations. The discourse is designed to generate some productive reflection among those inclined to reflect. This is the vital preliminary stage to effective action. The author of this essay has no axe to grind. He is simply a pilgrim in the vast sea of recorded knowledge. His purpose is to attempt to draw together the soundest counsel of recognized experts in various fields of study related to industrial relations and to present as objectively as possible, for the edification of interested laymen, a constructive analysis as to both the location and the nature of the fundamental controversies in this area.

The paper here presented was written by a student during his final year of work in the Marshall-Wythe School of Law in the College of William and Mary at Williamsburg, Virginia. The author, whose prior education embraced graduate work in the fields of naval architecture and management, feels obliged to acknowledge his considerable indebtedness to the faculties of each of the fine institutions it was his privilege to attend, William & Mary, the Naval Postgraduate School and George Washington University, because the patterns of thought peculiar to each field of study were essential to him in this undertaking. From architecture came recognition of the vital importance of an overall design which placed proportional emphasis on each of the component parts; from management came appreciation of the necessity in such communications for clarity, simplicity and conciseness; from the Law came an understanding of the powerful influence of history, of precedent and of political expedience.

On a more personal basis two primary sources of assistance deserve special mention; first, Miss Spotswood Hunnicutt, the Virginia historian, (now Mrs. Catesby G. Jones) whose vigorous criticism and careful proofreading was a major contribution; and secondly, my patient wife, whose invaluable secretarial assistance was the *sine qua non.* The author must also acknowledge extensive reliance on the current works from which he has quoted with the kind permission of the authors, respectively Professors Ludwig von Mises of New York University, Archibald Cox and Edward S. Mason of Harvard, and Eugene V. Rostow, Dean of the Yale Law School. The ideas set forth as a solution to the central problem, however, are borrowed from no one. These duly evolved from class room discussions stimulated by Professor James P. Whyte's excellent sessions in Labor Law at the Marshall-Wythe School in the College of William and Mary.

JOHN M. COURT

Williamsburg, Va.
November 1961

I.

AN OUTLINE OF THE TASK

As result of policies of deliberate design persistently pursued since the early days of the Great Depression we today find our economy host to a vast, rich, and aggressive labor cartel. What purposes it continues to serve and why we planned it this way are matters oft forgot amid the periodic anguish over how to handle our assertive guests. This situation has now achieved an institutional status, which the present generation accepts as an inevitable part of the scene, like the weather, alternately benign and foreboding.

One eminent and perceptive observer, the Harvard economist Sumner Slichter, scanning this state of affairs fifteen years ago, drew a sharp profile of the American labor movement, identifying in it these prominent characteristics:[1]

a) Tremendous power—big unions are "the most powerful economic organizations the country has ever seen."

b) Professional leadership—the leaders of the movement are full time professionals, "as remote from the rank and file as are the heads of large corporations."

c) Concentration of power within each union—"any competition for office at the national level is ruthlessly suppressed."

d) Intensive rivalry—rivalry, rather than economic considerations, guides union policy.

e) Specialized objectives—the movement is "characterized by strong particularisms and by lack of an organization which represents labor as a whole."

f) Failure to recognize the public interest—the trade union movement has failed to "adjust itself to the increasingly important role of government in determining conditions of employment."

Despite the subsequent nominal merger of the American Federation of Labor and the Congress of Industrial Organizations, achieved in 1955, the eventful intervening years have little changed the character of union power. Legislation enacted to abate its intemperance and stabilize its growth has tended primarily to consolidate its position.

The ramifications of union power are as pervasive as the ramifications of the economy itself. Beyond its immediate and obvious economic implications we may trace its significant impact on the political, sociological and even psychological aspects of American society.

We examine then a problem as infinitely complex as our society, a problem of the national spirit as well as of the economic body, of the federal will as much as of the electoral flesh. Accordingly it is the plan of this paper to review as comprehensively as the essay form permits:

a) The main historical currents which have brought us to the present state of labor affairs.

b) The formal rules of conduct which now apply to industrial relations; namely, what are the main features of Law applicable to labor and to the power of unions?

c) The problem of morale, of the spirit and the will; what are the incentives of labor and of unionism?

What indeed are the purposes of our federal society, if any, and how do they impinge on labor?

d) The economic problem posed by union power. What is the real context in which the forces and rules we have identified must operate? How is our economy supposed to be controlled and what has served to confound that control?

Indeed a large order, more than a life's work unless we rigidly ration our time and our effort, and objectively confine ourselves to the essentials with minimum detail or elaboration. After calling for the testimony of historians and legislators, of workers and managers, of economists and judges and then weighing the balance of the evidence, perhaps we can suggest how best to protect a free society's interest in its own continued well-being.

---

[1] *The Challenge of Industrial Relations,* Cornell University Press, 1947, 14-18.

He that would know what shall be, must consider what hath been.

H. G. Bohn: Handbook of Proverbs, 1855

11.

HISTORICAL PERSPECTIVE OF AMERICAN LABOR

Arnold Toynbee after analyzing the rise and fall of twenty civilizations, observes significantly:[1]

> The conclusion to which this retrospective reconnaissance brings us is that in the histories of civilization standardization is the master-tendency of the process of disintegration, in antithesis to the differentiation which we have found at an earlier point to be the master-tendency of the process of growth. And this conclusion is only what we should expect *a priori.* For if differentiation is the natural outcome of a succession of successful responses to a series of different challenges, standardization is no less manifestly the natural outcome of a succession of unsuccessful responses to a single challenge which monotonously continues to present itself so long as it thus remains unanswered.

Toynbee found a constant cycle of challenge and response throughout the recorded histories of each of the major distinguishable cultures of mankind which we call civilizations. Only that of the West is yet with us, a successor to that of the Greco-Roman and Judaic eras. While America itself is not to be confused with the ill-defined total entity of Western civilization, we certainly are a significant segment of it, and the pattern of phase relationships found by Toynbee in the great societies of the past will haunt us throughout our study.

Fundamentally what has happened in the growth period of each civilization is that its members' ingenuity and intelligence have devised satisfactory solutions to local problems without "passing the buck" to central authority. When the problems of a society are not resolved close to their point of origin, but are merely passed along and deposited on a central authority until the pressure becomes great enough to force immediate action, standardization begins to develop. In civilizations, or major societies, a general ennui of mind and spirit marks the end of growth just as in individuals. Thereafter its component social institutions begin to atrophy.

Relinquishing decisional responsibility to a remote central authority has become almost a national passion here since the outset of the New Deal. Discouragement of diversity and pressure for uniformity have risen steadily. We have witnessed an insidious and pervasive acceptance of standardization as an easy way out of local problems. Admiral Radford was struggling against the tide when as chairman of the Joint Chiefs of Staff during the aftermath of the unification controversy he somewhat acidly observed that standardization for the sake of standardization was the fetish of small minds. Our increasing intolerance of non-conformity is a mark of regression. Our loss of interest in self-determination reflects a dwindling vigor. Accordingly we should question whether coerced unionization or centralized administration of employment relationships throughout the country is a healthy or effective solution to the challenge industrialization offers our society. To put these issues in proper perspective we need to glance at some frequently overlooked history.

A notable challenge to Western civilization issued in the eighteenth century. Rigidly structured social and mercantile regimes had for centuries dominated the political and economic life of England, France and Spain. Ultimately these regimes were confronted at home with increasingly unruly populations which had outrun a primitive agricultural economy, and abroad with the necessity of organizing rapidly growing societies overseas upon which depended the vital inflow of new wealth to the homeland. The traditional social structures obviously were inadequate to manage, for long, either situation.

The most successful responses made to this challenge developed concurrently in England and her American colonies. Cromwell's revolution had broken the feudal pattern and radically new departures could be made. Accordingly responsibility and initiative were passed down from a land-holding aristocracy to an aggressive citizenry, and gradually the government's role became confined to essentially police functions. Monopolistic commercial institutions which had been the primary tools of Mercantilism for exploration and development overseas were abandoned for a more flexible trading pattern. Two men, Adam Smith and Thomas Jefferson, brilliantly influenced this crucial era of Anglo-American history, and best exemplified the most successful response made in the West to the challenge. They deserve more than passing note here. Concepts and doctrines with which they stirred and inspired their contemporaries became indelibly inscribed on the institutions of generations to follow.

Adam Smith was publishing in London his masterpiece *An Inquiry into the Nature and Causes of the Wealth of Nations* at the same time that Thomas Jefferson in Philadelphia was converting his pamphlet *A Summary View of the Rights of America* into the *Declaration of Independence*. The fullness of time had come. The stage was set for the advent of a progressive series of revolts against the old order. England had broken through the initial barriers to industrialization. A population of more than seven million overtaxed her lands. Her high-seas foes, Holland, Spain and France had bowed to superior British naval prowess. Africa, the Indies, and the Americas with all their incalculable wealth beckoned beyond open oceans. The moment was ripe for sufficiently courageous and resourceful entrepreneurs to seize opportunity by the forelock. The epigram of the age was that coined by a pioneer French industrialist who, when asked by the King's Minister what the government could do to help, replied emphatically "Laissez nous faire."—literally —"Leave to us the doing!"[2]

Adam Smith was a Scotsman, a professor of logic and jurisprudence. A keen practical observer and diligent researcher, with a genius for the orderly assembly of a vast variety of data, he did not so much originate theory as to gather together the best thinking of a fertile period and put it in cohesive form. As Einstein in a later century was to pull together from fragmentary discoveries by brilliant contemporaries a comprehensive reformulation of the relationships and principles of the physical world, so Smith in his day put together in the then pre-eminent field of philosophical interest, political economy, a master blueprint of the social order for launching the Industrial Revolution.

The Wealth of Nations declared that labor is the real measure of the value, in exchange, of all commodities; that the annual labor of a nation is the source from which is derived its total supply of necessities and conveniences of life. (Here lay the original concept of Gross National Product). The improvement of productivity of labor depends primarily upon its degree of specialization. Specialization will expand in ratio to the full breadth of the market offered. Hence the secret of a continuing increase in productivity lies in a steadily expanding market, and the secret of national opulence is a world-wide exchange. The specialization of labor implies that everyone must exchange for what he himself needs and wants. As more of what everyone requires is obtained by exchange, the more the market is enlarged. It is the wide exchange of goods which gives meaning to the concept of value. "Equal quantities of labor have equal value at all times and places to the laborer." "Labor alone, never varying in its own value, is the ultimate and real standard by which the value of all commodities can at all times and places be estimated and compared."[3] The vital importance of the productivity of the worker finally had received proper recognition in the scheme of political economy.

Whereas Adam Smith was designing for the Industrial Revolution, Jefferson and his colleagues were laying the foundation for a new approach to the exercise of popular sovereignty. The two pieces of construction, though distinctly diverse in substance and purpose, were founded upon a common philosophy and would ultimately become inextricably interconnected.

Thomas Jefferson was an erudite son of the frontier, a practical man of extraordinary intellectual curiosity, unafflicted with false pretensions, "the most conspicuous of American apostles of democracy, and one of the great liberals of modern times."[4]

His own scale of values was succinctly revealed in the epitaph he drafted for himself: "Here was buried Thomas Jefferson, author of the American Declaration of Independence, of the Statute of Virginia for religious freedom, and father of the University of Virginia."

We are concerned here not with the story of the life of Thomas Jefferson, but in the doctrine he espoused and the spirit he infused in the endless host of adherents following him into the mainstream of American life. After early success in the practice of law Jefferson undertook the more satisfying career of public servant. Of lawyers he observed in retrospect with the asperity of an architect and builder, they "question everything, yield nothing and talk by the hour."[5] Of government, he wrote, after almost fifty years of strenuous public responsibility,[6] "Societies exist under three forms: without governments, as among our Indians; under governments wherein the will of everyone has just influence; under governments of force. It is a problem not clear in my mind that the first is not the best."

This seeming digression is pressed upon the reader for this reason: because Smith in England and Jefferson here, through the confidence they radiated in the vigor of a free society, together succeeded in unleashing throughout the English-speaking world an unparalleled burst of constructive energy. With unanswerable logic they demanded the diffusion of authority and the distribution of responsibility throughout the whole of the political economy. Today, amid our evermore complicated efforts at governmental management, it is essential that we reconsider and re-evaluate an equally confident approach to the challenges besetting us.

Smith was primarily concerned with economic well-being, Jefferson primarily with our social well-being. Smith's chief reliance was placed on the maintenance of open competition in manufacturing and commerce. The mainspring of Jefferson's concept lay in the encouragement of personal independence, education, and agriculture. Both men were intimately acquainted with the sinister restrictions of a politically rigged economy. Each by the same philosophy sought to free the tremendous ingenuity and constructive energy they witnessed in a resourceful citizenry.

Smith thus defined the function of government:[7]

> According to the system of natural liberty, the sovereign has only three duties to attend to; three duties of great importance, indeed, but plain and intelligible to common understandings.
>
> First: the duty of protecting the society from the violence and invasion of other independent societies.
>
> Secondly: the duty of protecting as far as possible, every member of society from the injustice or oppression of every other member of it, or the duty of establishing the exact administration of justice.
>
> Thirdly: the duty of erecting and maintaining certain public works and public institutions which it can never be for the interest of any individual, or small number of individuals, to erect and maintain because the profit would never repay the expense to any individual or small number of individuals, though it may frequently do much more than repay it to a great society.

The political philosophy of the Jeffersonian State could not have been more cogently summarized.

Against this background of basic principles, let us examine some of the give and take which took place at the practical level after the great experiment in freedom was undertaken here in 1776. The Articles of Confederation formalized the authority of the existing emergency wartime Congress. This government was scarcely more authoritative, in a relative sense, than the North Atlantic Treaty Organization is today. No money could be raised on its own authority to pay its debts nor to carry on its responsibility for the common defense. Internal freedom of trade was thwarted by state rivalry, by erratic currency values and inflation, and by a shortage of capital or credit. Economic chaos resulted. In 1787 a Constitutional Convention of about fifty seasoned men was assembled to devise modifications to the Articles of Confederation which would resolve the immediate problems. Political theory had to give way to economic reality. It was determined that the alliance would be replaced with a formally structured federal organization of limited authority spelled out in a new contract between the independent states. By the new contract between the young states freedom of internal trade would be assured; currency would be standardized; authority for the regulation of commerce would be confined to the federal Congress, in which an independent taxing authority also was recognized. Individual approval by each member of the Confederation was necessary and was finally grudgingly obtained. With our new Federal Republic we thus began again in the year of tumultuous revolution in France.

For our federal system the violent repercussions of the events in France in 1789 did not begin to subside until after Waterloo in 1815. By this time, although the progress of our political experiment had been seriously impeded, the Jeffersonian State had become firmly established. There followed a decade of "good feeling," but by 1825, after the twenty-four year hegemony of the "Virginia Dynasty," three major economic interests had emerged from the free market arena established under the Constitution.

These three economic interests, forerunners of modern "pressure groups," comprised that of the slave holders who sought paradoxically to maintain a free market for exchange of their agricultural products, that of the nascent industrial communities of the Northeast who demanded tariff protection, and those of the public lands speculators along the frontier who insisted on federal assistance to accelerate the development of the Western territories.

Labor as a distinguishable political force remained submerged until late in the nineteenth century because each of these three forces effectively swallowed up its related labor interest. In the South, aside from the basically independent nature of agricultural communities, the rising external political pressure of the Northern and Western groups made it a matter of honor for the free population to stand together for the freedom of the market and for freedom from federal domination. Labor in the industrially inclined Northeast was constantly being replaced with new blood from abroad while most of the older hands went West to gain fortunes in the free lands. The elements of earlier stock who remained on the scene waxed prosperous behind the tariff protection afforded new industry and further profited from the general increase in population and in investment which raised values of local property. Labor in the West along the frontier had aspirations of independence and early prosperity which erased conventional class distinctions. So long as Calhoun, Webster and Clay dominated the Senate, each epitomizing the interest of his respective pressure group but personally mindful of the halcyon days of the great republic, the showdown was postponed and the blurred hope of sustaining the government of classic liberalism visualized by Smith and Jefferson lived on.

When a new generation succeeded the great triumvirate in the Senate the centrifugal forces exerted by the three pressures overcame the once dominant concept of limited government. After the complete destruction of the South in 1865, the vindictive industrial interests of the North could uninhibitedly enlarge and entrench a long series of their profitable projects. This led to such uncontrolled excesses that the once submerged or enveloped labor interests finally began to speak up for themselves. By 1877, when the army of occupation in the South was finally recalled, a national labor movement of significance had gathered, and had shown its strength, with attendant violence, in a widespread strike of railway workers protesting wage reductions.[8]

Not surprisingly, the first political impact of labor was felt in the West. In California where tens of thousands of Chinese had been imported by eastern industrialists to build railroads at wages Americans could not accept, a workers' political party was formed to combat immigration of Chinese and to forbid Orientals from acquiring land in California. Sympathetic reaction elsewhere by a growingly conscious labor electorate led to the passage of the first Chinese Exclusion Act[9] in 1882.

About this time a national labor organization called the Knights of Labor had generated among a group of garment-cutters in Philadelphia.[10] To avoid reprisals it had begun as a secret order intended to improve market conditions and employment situations through consumer-producer cooperation. The movement unveiled itself publicly in 1881 and offered its planned haven for labor in the period of rapid expansion of industrial organization. The objectives of the Knights included public ownership of public utilities and banks, compulsory arbitration of industrial disputes, and formation of a single national union including all crafts, skills, professions, sexes, and races. Membership was open to all except lawyers, bankers, gamblers, brokers and liquor dealers! [11] Fundamentally the Knights sought to substitute a vast structure of cartels in place of the open market for labor and commodities. By 1886, in the movement's heyday, it comprised almost three quarters of a million members, but its heterogeneous character proved a fatal weakness.

In the same year a different sort of labor movement achieved prominence. Its leading figure was a cigar maker named Samuel Gompers and its technique was more pedestrian and pragmatic. It sought the coordination of local craft unions, each with substantial autonomy in its organization, management and negotiations, each concentrating its membership in a special skill or trade. Thus began the now familiar American Federation of Labor. It soon became and has steadily remained the solid core of the labor movement.

The notorious activity of the industrial barons during this period aroused so much public concern, particularly with regard to railroad operations, that two landmark statutes in the economic field were enacted by a hesitant Congress. The public had finally become aware that Pandora's box had been opened by the use of governmental favor to facilitate the formation of great concentrations of wealth. Partisan protectionism, vast land subsidies to the railroad builders, and uncontrolled corporate conspiracy and speculation aimed at control of markets showed how the public interest could be abused through such powerful economic leverage. In 1887 the Interstate Commerce Act[12] was passed declaring illegal some of the more vicious competitive and collaborative techniques with which the public had been fleeced by the railroads. The first quasi-judicial body to administer such legislation was established thereby, the Interstate Commerce Commission. Thus began the long and complex history of active centralized regulation of commerce by our federal government. Three years later in 1890, the Sherman Antitrust Act[13] was enacted to discourage rigging the market against the public interest. The machinations of railroads and of the oil interests had convincingly demonstrated the evil power of unsupervised corporate maneuvers among property holders. That ingenious invention of the law, the corporation, had through governmental neglect and political favor become a frightening menace, and the electorate demanded protection.

It is important to note carefully this bifurcation of federal policy which took place in the formative years of industrialization. Two main techniques were initially selected for exercising the economic responsibility assumed by the federal government—the active or regulatory approach, emphasizing the special administrative agency, and the defensive or liberal approach, as spelled out in Adam Smith's second precept of governmental functions, judicially protecting the various members of society from the oppression of its transgressors. The railroads, generously stimulated by public largess, had taken on the aspect of a public utility. The federal government relied directly upon them in operating the mail system and in national defense. Through the regulatory approach the government acquired an active share in their management. The anti-trust laws on the other hand were fundamentally a federal codification of the common law with an additional specific assignment of responsibility for defense of the public interest in its larger sense.[13a]

At this opening stage of public concern over the power of concentrated capital, labor unions as a separate element for federal consideration were comparatively only a spot on the horizon. Later on, as our industrial labor force grew to a sizeable fraction of the total electorate and acquired influence politically therein, the two methods of federal economic management were to be specially adapted to accommodate the interests of labor. Originally, however, both the regulatory bodies and the anti-trust legislation were inspired by the antisocial conduct of the managers of industrial enterprise and were designed to protect the public interest, not to advance a private one.

By subsequent regulatory legislation many independent administrative agencies were established.[14] These had authority to draw up a vast body of administrative law, in which they functioned to considerable degree as judge, jury, and prosecutor in order to develop and enforce the specific public policy designated by Congress to be their respective functions. The anti-monopoly legislation, by contrast, began with exceedingly vague prohibitions against collusion in restraints of trade and against monopolies and conspiracies which could effect such restraints. Prosecution was left to the local District Attorney. Private parties injured by the violations had a right of action at law. The federal District Court with jurisdiction of the parties was the enforcement tribunal. The judiciary was counted on to make explicit the general intent of the Congress in enacting the law.

Given this latitude under the Sherman Act the courts quite logically determined that restraints of trade and monopolies exercised by labor organizations were quite as onerous to the public interest as were the conspiracies of the propertied gentlemen who pooled their resources and connived with one another to control the distribution, the price structure, or the available supply of certain products.

In the first great labor crisis after enactment of the antitrust laws, the federal judiciary, acting in defense of the public interest, acquired the deep distrust of union labor who thereafter persistently demanded the transfer of judicial functions in industrial disputes to more politically amenable regulatory agencies. This crisis occurred in 1894 when the patronizing personnel policies of the Pullman Company coupled with the wage reductions it adopted to cope with the current economic decline induced large numbers of their employees to organize in a local chapter of the rapidly growing American Railway Union.[15] The Pullman Company reacted with discriminatory discharges of union members. The local union countered the discharges with a strike. The issue remained stalemated several months until the national organization of the Railway Union held a convention in Chicago at which representatives of its 465 locals and the 150,000 members voted to assist their Pullman brethren by a boycott of all Pullman cars on all railroads. In the meantime the railroads had developed a coordinating body, the General Managers Association, which took counter-measures against the boycott, hiring protective and replacement personnel and firing the boycotters. The union expanded the strike to enforce the boycott. This resulted in widespread violence. Finally, the U. S. Circuit Court acting on a complaint from the Attorney General at the instance of President Cleveland issued an injunction under the Sherman Anti-trust Act forbidding any further interference with the operation of mail trains. The injunction was disregarded. Federal troops were dispatched over the protest of the Governor of Illinois to halt the interference. The Union's leaders were seized on warrants for contempt of court and the strike was thus broken. Eugene Debs the leader of the rail union and a great rival of Gompers, was convicted of the contempt charge.[16] Debs later became a socialist and remained a highly controversial but influential figure. The industry-wide union had shown its potency.

Out of this melee a formal investigating group, the United States Strike Commission, after an objective search for facts, developed recommendations which became the foundation of positive labor law. The recommendations were:

a) that a permanent Mediation Board be established to recommend settlements after investigation,

b) that employers cease discrimination against union membership in employment contracts,

c) that unions be recognized by employers as entities entitled to represent employees.

Initially the federal government's frame of interest in industrial relations lay only in the railroads. Ultimately a parallel system was to be developed to encompass "interstate commerce" in its broadest interpretation.

The Erdman Act[17] in 1898 attempted to promulgate the recommendations of the Commission into law effective in the interstate railroads. The effort to enforce the Act ran afoul of constitutional guarantees of liberty and property[18] and therefore remained relatively ineffectual until reinforced by additional legislation and a change of outlook in the Supreme Court. It is to be remembered, however, as the first national labor legislation. It established the precedent, unfailingly followed ever since by the Congress, that the transportation field is unique in its problem of labor relations and therefore is to be handled separately from other labor problems. Theoretically the objective of freedom of commerce had prompted congressional action rather than sympathy for the working man. The Erdman Act failed its purpose because the courts placed higher priority on the due process of law requirement of the Fifth Amendment than on the economic objectives of Congress.

Since the labor groups had enthusiastically backed the antitrust legislation they were deeply chagrined to find themselves "hoist on their own petard" in the Pullman strike. The basic difficulty was that the economic warfare tactics of labor organizations were of necessity so open and obvious as compared with the subtle and covert maneuvers of capital that the antitrust laws were very much more readily employed against labor than against capital. Courts could plainly observe the effect of mass picketing and strike violence whereas market rigging, like tax dodging, took extensive investigation to identify and was often extremely difficult to prove first-hand. These unfortunate circumstances led to the emotional popular conclusion that the courts were biased against labor and resulted in continuous agitation to exempt labor from judicial intervention.[19] The Clayton Act[20] was passed for this and other purposes. Gompers, who in the interim had been held in contempt of court himself,[21] hailed it as "Labor's Magna Carta."[22] This characterization proved overly hopeful for reasons we shall later examine. It took the Great Depression to produce the special immunity from legal process which labor wanted.

The eighteen year interim between the Clayton Act and the Norris-LaGuardia Act[23] saw the most significant labor history made in the rail industry. A war emergency measure, the Federal Control Act of 1918, gave the management of all railroad operations to the government. Secretary of Treasury McAdoo was assigned as Director-General of the Railroad Administration which, though leaving ownership in private hands, coordinated both personnel policy and operations. Unionization was recognized and fostered by the government but wages were held down. The result was that after the war when emergency management was relinquished the companies were faced with strong unions throughout their establishments and with vigorous demands for wage adjustments foregone in the war. The postwar depression caused the companies to seek wage reductions before the Railroad Labor Board, set up in 1920 under an amendment to the Interstate Commerce Act. The reductions were approved. A major strike followed in 1922 participated in by the shopmen but not by the operating unions. Again much violence ensued. Despite the Clayton Act over three-hundred local injunctions were issued in an effort to control the forcible interference with rail operations. Ultimately the U. S. Attorney General procured from a federal court a comprehensive temporary injunction against all the striking unions to prohibit their further interference with rail operations. The evidence of union inspired violence was so wide-spread and notorious that public opinion was effectively mobilized behind the employers. The strike soon thereafter came to an unsuccessful end.

The rail unions lost the battle but not the war.[24] They began immediately an all-out lobbying campaign to completely overhaul the law. Notably aided by the Progressive presidential candidate, Senator Robert La Follette, and by Representative Alben Barkley of Kentucky, a new Railway Labor Act[25] was finally passed in 1926. The hated Railroad Labor Board was abolished and elaborate arrangements were provided for mediation of disputes to avoid strikes. The employees' rights to union organization, independent of company domination, and the collective bargaining principle were formally recognized. The long sad subsequent financial and labor history of the railroads has led to a general impression that this legislation was not very satisfactory although certainly there were many other influences affecting the decline of the railroads. Suffice it to say, labor here learned the fine art of political finesse. The passage of the Railway Labor Act in the period of complete conservative domination of the federal government was an extraordinary piece of practical politics. Labor's lesson in politics had been learned and this skill it used well in the years to come.

With Franklin Roosevelt's dramatic entrance into the presidency the labor interest acquired a dominant position in national policy-making from which it has never retreated. The first attempt of the new administration to improve the state of the economy was primarily psychological. The primary objective of the National Industrial Recovery Act[25a] was the assurance of economic security. Codes of fair dealing were established administratively for each industry through collaboration of the NRA administrator with heads of major industrial firms. Minimum wages and maximum hours were codified. Labor organization was encouraged throughout industry. Price controls and market allocations were developed to prevent cutthroat competition. Briefly, a massive cartel system with a labor voice in management was devised, covering over seven-hundred recognized industries. Agriculture and mining were encompassed by similar legislation.[26]

This whole approach to our economy smacked strongly of the Mercantilism which Smith and his liberal cohorts had overwhelmed one-hundred and fifty years before. It was so diametrically contrary to the free competitive system upon which the federal republic had been nurtured that despite the extraordinary economic circumstances in which this remedy had been conceived, it could not be digested by the traditional legal system. In decision after decision,[27] as segments of the plan were challenged legally, the Supreme Court ruled the scheme unconstitutional. Faced with what he conceived to be the necessity of reconstructing the entire political, economic, and social foundations of the country, Mr. Roosevelt decided upon organized labor as the Trojan Horse with which to breach the walls of the competitive economy built to the plans of Smith and Jefferson, the judicial principles of which had frustrated the New Deal's primary strategy.

Thus the Wagner Act[28] in 1935, passed to salvage the basic impetus of the unconstitutional NIRA, gave labor unions virtual *carte blanche:* letters of marque and reprisal to raid, seige and pillage their economic enemy, corporate enterprise, in the name of the New Deal. They undertook their assignment with evident relish and great success. Between 1935 and 1945 the membership in labor unions rose from 3.7 million to 15 million, from 6% of the work force to 22%. For the professional union man the millenium had arrived. During the same decade the number of active corporations actually declined more than 10% and the value of their capital assets had shrunk over 8%.[29] Economic expansion had been at the government's expense. By 1946 the time had come for some changes to be made.[30]

It should be apparent to the reader at this point that the United States in its effort to cope with corporate power had in reality backed into the problem of union power. When corporate concentrations were first revealing their dangerous potential, labor was not a significant or distinct political entity. Congress exercised its authority over interstate commerce for the purpose of assuring better protection of the public interest in the economy. First in the railroad complex, which formed the matrix of our rapid industrialization, there was established a permanent monitor, the Interstate Commerce Commission. Then the federal judicial system was directed to defend the public against major economic conspiracies. The latter procedure was found to impinge on labor's measures of self-defense. Special privileges were then devised to protect union activity from both judicial and employer discrimination. Finally with the Great Depression came the Keynesian concept of economics which reasoned that the economy could only be revitalized by accelerating the circulation of national income.[31] The key step in utilizing the Keynesian concept lay in invigorating the unions so as to enable them to demand greater income for a large portion of the economy which labor, as a consumer, would promptly spend, and thus enlarge the Gross National Product. This theoretically would absorb the idle capacity of industry, increase employment, increase profits, increase re-investment of capital, and increase the tax take of the government, thus paying it back for the initial cost of pump priming.

Although Keynesian economic principles failed in the first two terms of Mr. Roosevelt's administration to pull the country out of its economic doldrums, the hitherto inconceivable expenditures of World War II produced results.[32] Some faithful Keynesians reasoned that their error had been that they had been too parsimonious. The Keynesian tools survived their owner's ascendency, however. Though the economic outlook at the conclusion of World War II was radically different from what it had been ten years before, when the Wagner Act had been passed, this depression-born charter of special privileges for unions remained the core of labor law. There also remained the complicated paraphernalia designed in the attempt to control rents, prices, production, allocations and crops. Virtually blotted out were the free market concepts of Smith and Jefferson.

After Roosevelt's death in 1945 the rampant

growth of regulatory agencies and their functions was recognized by both Attorney General Clark and the Congressional Judiciary Committees to necessitate more formalized requirements.[33] An attempt was made to codify and stabilize the field of administrative law. The Administrative Procedures Act,[34] passed in 1946, effected this purpose. This Act required systematic publication of administrative regulations, called for the employment of judicial procedures in the regulatory agencies, and established a procedure for the appeal of certain of their determinations, via the regular judicial system. In short, the way was pointed out. The doing was yet to be done.

It remains a very difficult, constantly recurring task to make the procedures of the regulatory agencies conform to basic concepts of Anglo-American jurisprudence and democratic federal government. In 1959 Eugene Victor Rostow, Dean of the Yale Law School, after a comprehensive study of the legal devices for management of the economy, stated in his book *Planning For Freedom*:[34a]

> I regard the law of regulated industries as one of the most urgent fields for research and reform in the whole of our law dealing with economic affairs. The present role of the state and federal regulatory agencies controlling railroads, utilities and the transportation and communications fields raise fundamental questions of both substance and procedure. The statutes they seek to enforce are usually out of date, often confusing, ill-drawn and needlessly complex. Many of the rules echo forgotten battles and guard against dangers which no longer exist. They comprise vast codes understood only by a jealous priesthood which protects these swamps and thickets from all prying eyes. The basic theme in the reform of these complex

charters should be to release the regulated industries as fully as circumstances permit.

It is the contention of this paper that the same general theme is applicable in the area of labor law and general trade regulation. The conversion from a war economy to what was fondly hoped would be a peace-time economy presented the really monumental task in governmental reorganization, one which appears never to have gotten far beyond the study stage. From 1945 to 1950 the bitter protracted struggle over military "unification" appears to have seriously distracted legislative as well as public attention from what was actually a more consequential and difficult administrative problem, that of consolidating and coordinating the multifarious federal salients projecting into the civilian economy.[35] Here the task is to halt the constant re-enactment of the saga of Penelope's web, one outfit laboriously unravelling by night what another with equal zeal had woven by day. The constant straining at cross purposes has been nowhere more evident than in the labor and antitrust fields where the whole effort on one hand sought to integrate industry and eliminate competition while the other sought persistently to fragment industry and accentuate competition.

Certainly each unit of industry, to compete in the strenuous modern international economy, must have close coordination of its own facilities, operations, and labor force. The Taft-Hartley Act[35a] of 1947 and its recent supplement the Landrum-Griffin Act[36] of 1959 have reflected congressional recognition of the prior imbalance in the governmental role in industrial relations. The growth of labor unions as a tool of government appears to have ended. Skirmishing will continue on the meaning of the law, but the present political situation indicates continued stalemate on its major features. It is possible to say now, fourteen years after a balanced regulatory scheme for industrial relations was enacted by the federal government, that a fair trial has been given it. The question before us is whether the *status quo* is the kind of system which will produce the results we, the public, want. That in turn raises the antecedent questions, what results have we, and what did we want?

Thus we complete the survey of the main historical currents which have brought us to the present state of labor affairs. We began our discourse with a view of labor union power as discerned from the perspective of a most eminent teacher and respected economist, Dr. Slichter. The good professor, writing in 1958, made some further cogent observations on the position of trade unions in the American economy which pinpoint the obvious symptoms of continuing economic imbalance in our society:

> When teachers, librarians, scientists, government employees, young engineers, lawyers, doctors, other highly trained people, and farmers compare their earnings with the wages of workers on assembly lines no wonder they feel a sense of injustice. During the past ten years the hourly compensation of employees in private industry outside of agriculture has increased more than twice as fast as the productivity of labor in all private industry outside of agriculture.[37]

Such is the disturbing situation which confronts us today. Thirty years ago we undertook to raise up a countervailing force to concentrated corporate power. That end is now achieved. A growing monolithic regulatory government structure goes with it. These are the results of planned policy. Is the policy in error? Were its original objectives mistakenly selected? Or is the *status quo* the best practical solution among unhappy alternatives?

FOOTNOTES — II

[1] Arnold J. Toynbee, *A Study of History*, Oxford University Press, IV, 322.

[2] Legendre to Colbert, see *Encyclopedia Britannica* (1957 ed.), XIII, 598.

[3] *An Inquiry Into the Nature and Causes of the Wealth of Nations*, Modern Library Edition, Random House, 1937, 33.

[4] *Encyclopedia Britannica* (1957 ed.), XII, 986.

[5] *Ibid.*, 987.

[6] *Ibid.*, 989.

[7] *Wealth of Nations, op. cit.*, 651.

[8] For a lucid account of events of this period see Edward W. Martin (James D. McCabe) *The History of the Great Riots—A full History of the Molly Maguires*, National Publishing Company, Philadelphia, 1877, and Robert V. Bruce, *1877: Year of Violence*, Bobbs-Merrill Company, 1959.

[9] 22 Stat 58, Act of 6 May, 1882; for more detailed background see J. A. Rayback, *A History of American Labor*, Macmillan Company, 1959, 139-142.

[10] Albion G. Taylor, *Labor Problems and Labor Law*, Prentice-Hall, 1950, 265.

[11] *Ibid.*, 265.

[12] 24 Stat. 379 (1887), 49 U. S. Code, Sec. 1, *et seq.*

[13] Act of July 2, 1890, 26 Stat. 209, as amended 15 U. S. Code, Sec. 1.

[13a] See Judge Taft's opinion in United States v. Addyston Pipe and Steel Co., 85 F. 271, affirmed 20 S. Ct. 96 (1899).

[14] Primary regulatory units other than the Interstate Commerce Commission comprise the Federal Trade Commission, Security and Exchange Commission, Board of Governors of the Federal Reserve, Federal Communications Commission, Maritime Administration, Civil Aeronautics Board, and National Labor Relations Board.

[15] For a most comprehensive impartial study, see generally *Report on the Chicago Strike of June, July—1894, by the United States Strike Commission, appointed by the President July 26, 1894, under the provisions of Section 6 of Chapter 1063 of the Laws of the United States passed October 1, 1888*, U. S. Government Printing Office, 1895.

[16] United States v. Debs, 64 F. 724 (1894).

[17] 30 Stat. 424, Act of 1 June 1898.

[18] Adair v. U. S., 208 U. S. 161, 28 S. Ct. 277 (1908).

[19] See Samuel Gompers, "Judicial Labor-Phobia in Antitrust Law, Injunctions and Contempts," *American Federationist,* (June 1914) 453-466.

[20] 38 Stat. 730, Act of 15 October, 1914.

[21] Gompers v. Bucks Stove & Range Company, 221 U. S. 418 (1911).

[22] *American Federationist,* (July 1914) 553.

[23] 47 Stat. 70, Act of 23 March, 1932, 29 U. S. Code, Sec. 101-115.

[24] See Donald R. Richberg, *Labor Union Monopoly,* Regnery, 1957, 3-27.

[25] 44 Stat. 577, Act of 20 May, 1926, 45 U. S. Code, Sec. 151-163.

[25a] 48 Stat. 195, Act of 16 June, 1933.

[26] Agricultural Adjustment Act, 48 Stat. 31 (1933); Bituminous Coal Conservation Act, 49 Stat. 991 (1935).

[27] See Schechter v. United States, 295 U. S. 495 (1935); United States v. Butler, 297 U. S. 1 (1936); Carter v. Carter Coal Co., 298 U. S. 238 (1936).

[28] 49 Stat. 449, Act of 5 July, 1935, 29 U. S. Code, Sec. 151, *et seq.*

[29] See *Statistical Abstract of the United States* (1949), U. S. Department of Commerce: Table 384.

[30] In 1946 the elections for the 80th Congress gave the Republican party its only distinct control of the House and Senate exercised simultaneously in the period 1932-1961. The ratio of popular vote in the election was 53.5% Republican, and 44.3% Democratic. The House composition 245 Rep., 188 Dem.; the Senate 51 Rep., 45 Dem.; see tables 452 and 462, *Statistical Abstract of the United States* (1960).

[31] See generally: John Maynard Keynes, *A Treatise on Money* (1930), and *The General Theory of Employment, Interest and Money* (1936), New York: Harcourt, Brace & Company.

[32] See Table I, *Statistical Tables from the President's Economic Report, 1959;* e.g., GNP in 1930 was 91.1 billion of which 71 was for personal consumption and 9.2 was for governmental purchases of goods and services; in 1934 corresponding figures were 65.0, 51.9, 9.8; in 1939, 91.1, 67.6, 13.3; in 1944, 211.4, 109.8, 96.5.

[33] See U. S. Code Congressional Service, 79th Congress, 2d. Session, 1946, 1195-1206.

[34] 60 Stat. 237, Act of 11 June, 1946, 5 U. S. Code, Sec. 1001, *et seq.*

[34a] Yale University Press, 1959, 311.

[35] See generally: the so-called "Hoover Report," officially designated *Report of the Commission on Organization of the Executive Branch of the Government.* (1949).

[35a] 61 Stat. 136, 29 U. S. Code, Sec. 141-197 as amended, officially designated *Labor Management Relations Act.*

[36] 73 Stat. 519, officially designated *Labor Management Reporting and Disclosure Act of 1959*.

[37] *Labor in a Free Society,* University of California Press, 1959, 28. Dr. Slichter did not live to read the account of the Senate Subcommittee investigating the notorious wage scandals at the missile base sites, where under cost-plus contracts the building trades unions had run their weekly wage level in many cases to well over $600. These facts were disclosed generally to the press about 1 May, 1961.

Power, like a desolating pestilence,
Pollutes whate'er it touches.

P. B. SHELLEY: Queen Mab, III, 1813

III.

THE COMPLEX PATTERN OF EMPLOYMENT LAWS

Archibald Cox, while a Harvard law professor, testifying to the Senate Judiciary Committee in 1959 said,[1]

> . . . labor unions enjoy their present power by virtue of Federal statutes, chiefly the National Labor Relations Act. Other voluntary associations are different in two respects: (1) they lack the statutory power of a union designated as a bargaining representative; (2) no other voluntary association has as much power over an individual's livelihood and opportunities or over the rules governing his daily life. The union bulks much larger in the life of a worker than a corporation in the affairs of a stockholder.

The legal basis of union power is found in the immunities and privileges which attach by statute to labor union activities. The significance of these will be lost unless the reader keeps in mind, in general outline at least, the basic pattern of law into which these immunities or privileges are set.

By 1776 English common law had digested not only the old ecclesiastical law but a sort of international code developed over the centuries as special law for those engaged in commerce. Thus the colonies began their independent course with a cohesive body of judicial precedents comprehending all civil justice. Each citizen could protect his rights through the courts of law without aid of new legislation. If the absence of suitable precedent prevented adjudication at law or if action were needed in the cause of justice to forestall prospective rather than to remedy past transgressions, the complainant could petition the sovereign for special relief through courts of equity whereupon, on the more abstract basis of "natural law", the chancery court would determine a just solution in the circumstances proven and, upon an equitable decree or injunction, the officers of the court could enforce its determination. As our own statutory law developed, reliance on precedent and "natural law" declined and the major judicial function became the interpretation and adaptation of the expressed legislative will of the sovereign into a myriad of unique and frequently unanticipated situations. Nevertheless the common law concept of one code for all citizens and of equality before the bar of justice carried over into the statutes of the new government. The Comity Clause in the Articles of Confederation became the Privileges and Immunities Clause of the Constitution.[2] Their intent was to assure that all citizens enjoyed in the eyes of the law the same privileges and immunities. Government would proceed by impersonal law of general application. The fifth amendment in the Bill of Rights placed on the federal government substantially the same obligation to recognize the equal status of all citizens in the legal sense.[2a]

Labor law texts often cite a few scattered opinions[3] rendered in labor disputes in the early days of the federal republic as evidence of a general bias of the courts in favor of property owners and against labor. The cases reveal, however, a pattern of attempted coercion by the labor groups wherever the courts were assertive.[4] The great accomplishment of the common law had been the substantial elimination of bias of privilege and of special codes, digesting all into a balanced comprehensive system of marked stability which was accepted with grateful respect and keen understanding by the people at large. The common law back through the Middle Ages is replete with cases on trade regulation illustrating that the courts persistently struggled to maintain individual freedom of action.[5] Open or covert agreements to interfere with public access to open exchange was not only a tort, but such combinations in the eighteenth century were also penalized by statute law in England;[6] that is, Parliament declared it a punishable misdemeanor to conspire to effect a monopoly or a restraint of trade. The most onerous early monopolies were the result of Sovereign grants of special privilege and first occurred in royal patents. The abuse of these led to the sharp curtailment of royal power by Parliament.[7] Legalized monopolies thereafter took the form of corporations chartered by Parliament with a narrow delegation of sovereign powers for a specified purpose.

The corporation is a legal concept in which an unlimited number of persons may pool a part of their resources in a formal organization recognized at law as an entity separate from its members and clothed with many of the rights of citizenship. Its permanence, its limited liability, and its flexibility of ownership as well as some of its tax advantages have made the corporation a much greater power in the economy than the individual entrepreneur or proprietor. As industrialization expanded, our States gradually relaxed the formalities for creation of corporations so that by 1880 incorporation often no longer required a special act of the legislature but had become in many states a routine administrative procedure. Thereafter incorporators could write their own charters pretty much to suit themselves. The idea of forwarding a governmental purpose in the creation of corporations became lost except for a relatively small number of those government and municipal corporations still created by legislative act. Meanwhile the perpetuation of concentrated wealth in a family by trusts or by entail had been made very difficult by statute both in England and here. Modern estate and inheritance taxes will ere long complete the job of fragmenting family fortunes. The corporation meantime has steadily grown in economic importance. Professor Mason in *The Corporation in Modern Society* states:[8]

> The five hundred largest business corporations in this country embrace nearly two-thirds of all non-agricultural activity. These and similar figures are reiterated with such frequency that they tend to bounce off our heads rather than to penetrate. But by now we are all aware that we live not only in a corporate society but a society of large corporations. The management, that is, the control, of these corporations is in the hands of, at most, a few thousand men. Who selected these men, if not to rule over us, at least to exercise a vast authority, and to whom are they responsible? The answer to the first question is quite clear: they selected themselves. The answer to the second is at best nebulous. This, in a nutshell, constitutes the problem of legitimacy.

This language is also substantially true of national and international labor unions, except that labor's controlling hierarchy appears to be a smaller group, less inhibited by public scrutiny. Abram Cheyes, former Professor of Law at Harvard, lately counsel to the State Department, states in the same text: "They (the big corporations) are repositories of power, the biggest centers of non-governmental power in our society."[9] At the outset we noted a similar comment by Professor Slichter about labor unions. Such views are the basis for the doctrine of countervailing power which appears to dominate our present thinking in economic policy.[10]

The private corporation has gradually lost its original sovereign flavor but the labor union, once simply an association of artisans interested in maintaining the standards of skill in a given trade, has developed steadily into an important quasi-public institution. The reach of the private corporation, no longer accorded rights other than those possessed by individual citizens, can be delineated through the title to its property and the scope of its contracts. The union is a more nebulous entity and as a bargaining agent it acquires a distinct political authority and responsibility such that its power extends beyond the reach of its property, its membership, or the corporation or proprietorship in which the bargaining unit is located.[11]

The corporation, stemming from a royal institution, has always been formally organized, owing specific responsibilities to its creator, certain contractual obligations to its members, and possessed of distinct internal structure. It has taken many forms and been adapted to an extraordinary variety of common endeavors, the primary classifications of which being profit (stock), charity (non-stock), and municipal government. We have in every state a comprehensive body of law as to the conduct of corporations, well-expounded in judicial interpretation. Surprisingly, though corporations have long been the primary instruments of interstate commerce, we have no general federal corporation law. The Securities and Exchange Commission, the Federal Trade Commission, and other regulatory agencies take an active role in special areas, as when corporate securities are offered for public disposal, but the act of incorporation and the direct control of corporate conduct remains a state function.

Labor unions are not required to incorporate although there are various reasons advanced as to why such a requirement might be advisable, not the least of which is that it would standardize and simplify their legal treatment. Although a few unions have incorporated there are a few distinctions which in this country make the union *sui generis*. The union in its present role bears close resemblance to an ancillary municipal corporation, such as a transportation authority or a water district, in that it exercises special authority of a non-voluntary nature in a public function extraneous to the conventional subdivisions of government. Unions began simply as voluntary associations, not recognized as entities at law. Resembling at this stage a charitable group or fraternal lodge they were quite difficult to pin down to a contractual responsibility. This uncertainty of substance substantially explains the initial disinclination of management to deal with them; you could make an agreement with them but when you went to enforce it at law, you found yourself largely fanning the air. Responsibility was indistinct, membership was transient, and rarely was property attached. There was seldom any effective legal action available to a party aggrieved by a union other than to seek a preventive decree or judicial injunction from a court in equity because an award of damages usually proved uncollectable. Only the individuals could be sued at law; these had little property, and they could not be jailed for debt. For union misdeeds the only practicable remedy was a court order which said in essence to this nebulous group—"Don't do it again or we'll slap some bold fellow with contempt of court."

With this elementary explanation of prestatute labor law let us proceed to consider five major facets of union power from the standpoint of statutes now governing industrial relations:

(a) What is the role of the unions in the macroeconomic sphere? Why do they have special status in the maintenance of the national economy? These questions are vitally important because they furnish the *raison d'etre* of the original National Labor Relations (Wagner) Act[12] and the Norris-LaGuardia (Anti-Injunction) Act.[13] The authors of this legislation reasoned that only by improved communications between management and labor and by an improved distributing device for the national income could economic peace and prosperity be achieved. The union was imagined to be the perfect instrument for these purposes. Therefore its growth became a purpose of public policy high in priority.

(b) What is the position of the union in the microeconomic sense? How does the union exercise power over the community and vice versa? Here we encounter the effect of various immunities to conventional judicial procedure which, coupled with the doctrine of federal pre-emption, leave our component communities virtually powerless before an aggressive national union.

(c) Although the political stigma affixed to corporate wealth makes the average American apathetic to the tribulations of employers, our study cannot ignore the legal position of the harassed managements of industrial enterprise. Whether or not we sympathize with the captains of industry, the fact remains that the productivity of each worker depends in good measure upon the efficiency of his management and the amount of capital invested in the tools he uses. If the climate of the law fails to encourage either, we shall find ourselves steadily losing ground in world markets and in comparative economic strength.

(d) What is the status of the union at law *vis-a-vis* the individual worker? The federal government has come to consistently ignore or preempt the prerogatives of the state and community governments. The hapless industrial property owners have been chief quarry in an endless game of hare and hounds. Only the workers themselves appear to comprise a sufficiently significant element of the electorate to ultimately exercise corrective leverage on the federal political machinery. Their legal status is therefore quite important to our analysis.

(e) A fifth aspect can be touched on only briefly herein. This is the relationship of a local union with the national and international goliaths, the community organization versus the professionals who operate on a country-wide perspective. Were the antitrust immunities of the unions to be modified, this relationship might acquire great importance.

The macroeconomic role of unions developed from the economic theory adopted by President Roosevelt in his first administration. It had as its original premise the necessity for halting competition and ambitiously expanding the role of the federal government. Senator Wagner in presenting the National Labor Relations Act to the Senate on 1 March, 1934 offered the following explanation:[14]

> The keynote of the recovery program is organization and cooperation. Employers are allowed to unite in trade associations in order to pool their information and experience and make a concerted drive upon the problems of modern industrialism. If properly directed, this united strength will result in unalloyed good to the nation. But it is fraught with great danger to workers and consumers if it is not counterbalanced by the equal organization and equal bargaining power of employees. Such equality is the central need of the economic world today. It is necessary to insure a wise distribution of wealth between management and labor, to maintain a full flow of purchasing power, and to prevent recurrent depressions.

On May 27, 1935, the Supreme Court handed down the memorable decision of Schechter Poultry Corp. v. United States,[15] holding that the federal regulation of local trade under the National Industrial Recovery Act exceeded the delegated powers of Congress and violated the Tenth Amendment. This necessitated a reorientation of the justification for the measure proposed since the powers assigned to the federally sponsored trade associations to which Wagner had referred were thereby made unconstitutional. The modified justification, recited in the Act itself, as approved in July 1935 declared:[16]

> The inequality of bargaining power between employees who do not possess full freedom of association or actual liberty of contract and employers who are organized in corporate or other forms of ownership

association substantially burdens and affects the flow of commerce and tends to aggravate recurrent business depressions by depressing wage rates and the purchasing power of wage earners in industry and by preventing the stabilization of competitive wage rates and working conditions within and between industries.

Experience has proved that protection by law of the right of employees to organize and bargain collectively safeguards commerce from injury, impairment or interruption and promotes the flow of commerce by removing certain recognized sources of industrial strife and unrest, by encouraging practices fundamental to the friendly adjustment of industrial disputes arising out of differences as to wages, hours or other working conditions and by restoring equality of bargaining power between employers and employees.

When the emergency had passed, a postwar Congress added another paragraph under the above "Findings and Policies" of the National Labor Relations Act which read as follows:[17]

Experience has further demonstrated that certain practices by some labor organizations, their officers and members have the intent or the necessary effect of burdening or obstructing commerce by preventing the free flow of goods in such commerce through strikes and other forms of industrial unrest or through concerted activities which impair the interest of the public in the free flow of such commerce. The elimination of such practices is a necessary condition to the assurance of the rights herein guaranteed.

As Justice Holmes pithily observed, "The life of the law has not been logic; it has been experience."[18] It was the happy hope of the early depression Congresses that industrial strife would cease to plague the freedom of commerce if only employers were thwarted from interfering with unionization of their employees and were required to share control of their enterprises with these unions through "collective bargaining." The sponsors theorized that since this procedure would raise wages and stimulate consumption it would thereby accelerate growth of the overall economy, whereas otherwise the excess profits of industry would merely be salted away in "unproductive" savings.

Unions are an essential feature of an industrial economy. Their recognition as collective bargaining agents is a legal necessity, but as our subsequent discourse will develop, laws conferring exclusive privileges upon unions and segregating the system of law in the field of industrial relations from the basic judicial system of our federal society have overshot the mark at which they were purportedly aimed in spite of the corrections attempted in more recent legislation.

In the meantime the federal government has undertaken to stimulate the distribution of national income by important other means. It has elaborately built a floor of fair labor standards and wages,[19] cushioned it with social security of steadily increasing coverage and generosity,[20] sponsored comprehensive unemployment insurance and workmen's compensation acts,[21] underwritten vast housing outlays and given away mountains of comestibles to improve the lot of the low income bracket in our economy. For almost thirty years the federal legislative mills have steadily ground out welfare legislation which has engulfed the originally conceived economic function of the unions. To this fact Sumner Slichter referred in his sixth major union characteristic, their disregard of the increasing importance of the government's role.

Following the departure of Franklin Roosevelt from the national scene there came a reassessment of the basic policies of the federal government. Some fundamental legislation bordering on a constitutional nature was enacted in the early postwar years; the Administrative Procedures Act[22] and the Employment Act[23] were especially noteworthy. In the area of macroeconomics perhaps the most significant statement of policy is that set forth in the first section of the Employment Act of 1946 which reads thus:

> The Congress declares that it is the continuing policy and responsibility of the federal government to use all practicable means consistent with its needs and obligations and other essential considerations of national policy, the assistance and cooperation of industry, agriculture, labor and state and local governments, to coordinate and utilize all its plans, functions and resources for the purpose of creating and maintaining, in a manner calculated to foster and promote free competitive enterprise and general welfare, conditions under which there will be afforded useful employment opportunities, including self-employment, for those able, willing and seeking to work, and to promote maximum employment, production, and purchasing power.

That long awkward sentence, obviously hammered out painfully in legislative compromise, says a good deal and implies a great deal more. It is the mark of John Maynard Keynes on our faltering federalism. The federal government is declared responsible for the concentration of all its vast powers (1) upon the creation of conditions affording employment for those desiring it and (2) upon the acceleration of the national economy to the fullest extent practicable. Implicit is recognition that, rightly or wrongly, the federal government will be held responsible for any economic deceleration. Implicit also is recognition that the federally controlled section of the economy had reached such mammoth proportions as to make it essential that the exercise of this economic-flywheel function be open, above-board and official. The knowing observer could rightly reason that the necessary authority to discharge such a vast responsibility would be assumed by future Congresses, future administrations and future courts, the basic constitutional concept of a limited federal government and of latent reserved powers in the States to the contrary notwithstanding.

It is worthy of note that in the whole Constitution the only thread of connection between the economic responsibility set forth in the Employment Act and the basic authority granted to the federal government by the people of the States lies in that heavily trafficked clause under Article I, section 8 assigning to Congress power ". . . to regulate commerce with Foreign nations, among the several States, and with the Indian tribes."

An aggressive expansion of the meaning of the power to "regulate commerce . . . among the several States" has been undertaken by the judiciary since the start of Mr. Roosevelt's second term, after he broached his controversial plan to pack the Supreme Court. Their historic change in position was spelled out in 1937 in the Jones and Laughlin case[24] in which the application of National Labor Relations Board authority to a local employment controversy at a steel plant was upheld on the rationale that its production "affected" commerce and therefore was intended to be covered in the constitutional grant of implementing power to

Congress. This 5 to 4 decision substantially annulled the Ninth and Tenth Amendments and opened the legislative floodgates for the establishment of the welfare state.

The only real bounds of federal authority today in the economic field appear to lie in the inclination of the Congress framing the statute and in the zeal of the respective regulatory body for handling the workload entailed. To illustrate, the courts have declared the following workers to be encompassed by the federal power over interstate commerce: window-washers contracting to wash windows in an office building whose tenants do some interstate business,[25] employees of an ice plant whose customers occasionally carry ice out of the state,[26] workers on an irrigation ditch the water from which waters fields in which produce is raised to be sold out of state,[27] and office workers in a news service which collects news from out of state and distributes it locally.[28] The National Labor Relations Board is empowered to write its own ticket to the limits of federal jurisdiction in this field.[29]

Although the student may marvel that a responsibility such as that of the Employment Act with all its pervasive attendant authority could have been assumed without contemplation of any constitutional amendment, he should appreciate the fact that by 1946 the Congress, acting *ex post facto*, was conscientiously trying to spell out a restraint rather than an extension of federal responsibility, as is revealed in the Senate-House conference report with which the Act was finally presented:[30]

> The Senate declared that it is the responsibility of the federal government to maintain full employment and to assure at all times sufficient opportunities for

employment to enable all Americans able and willing to work to exercise their right to continued full employment.

The House substitute declared it is the continuing policy of the United States to promote employment, production and purchasing power under the system of free competitive enterprise and that the function of the government is to *promote and not to assure or guarantee employment.* It is the theory of the House substitute that employment is not the sole responsibility of the government and that industry, agriculture and labor have their responsibility. . . . The term 'full employment' is rejected and maximum employment is the objective to be promoted. . . . The United States is to promote by all practicable means which may well include, but need not be limited to taxation, banking, credit and currency, foreign trade, public works, loans. Studies are to be made and causes of economic dislocations ascertained. Causes of unemployment are to be removed or eliminated. The goal is maximum or high levels of employment; the emphasis on spending, expenditures and disbursements is omitted from the conference agreement.

Our traumatic experience in the Great Depression has been popularly attributed to a maldistribution of national income caused by an increasingly unbalanced concentration of economic power in big corporations. The cure prescribed was a cartelization of labor, industry, and agriculture followed by a grand scale collaboration with government to conduct a substantially planned economy. A generation of consolidation followed, after which gnawing doubts began to stir a deep concern as to the wisdom of encouraging such unwieldy concentrations of economic power. Meanwhile unintelligibly complex codes of regulatory law and interpretations have grown tier on tier acquiring a defense in depth almost beyond penetration short of revolution. Behind not the least of these citadels of verbosity stands the nationwide combine of organized labor.

The most significant attack on the *status quo* of union power comes now from the same academic quarter which thirty years ago insisted that the unions be put on the macroeconomic map in large letters. Economists now perceive an unbalance opposite to that which then tilted the economy heavily to one side.[31] The broad immunity so long extended to unions from restraints applicable to the other elements of our society has permitted and encouraged such a strong concentration and deep entrenchment of their collective power that they may ultimately prove more difficult to dislodge from political dominance than any prior vested interests. The unions' base is broader, their source of wealth more secure, their organization more compact, and their opposition more completely cowed.[32]

Let us therefore examine some of the unique union privileges and immunities which have made their economic power inaccessible to the normal processes of the law. In a practical sense what was accomplished by the Norris-LaGuardia Act and by the Wagner Act?

The Norris-LaGuardia Act of 1932 rigidly constrained the authority of the federal judiciary in labor disputes. The use of one of the basic tools of equity, the injunction, by the federal judiciary against union activity of any sort was almost wholly outlawed. A "labor dispute" was officially defined in the Act so broadly that union organizers actually representing no one in an industrial community, could, without any local occasion, instigate picketing under the protection of the act, and be held blameless for any resultant concerted violence or economic damage.[33] Thus the stranger picket and the secondary boycott were made inviolate in any industry with a scintilla of interstate activity. Neither the strike nor the boycott needed to involve any local employees or issues. National or international unions accordingly could project their activities nationally without need of reasonably persuading a significant number of employees to join, or finding any conflict between labor and management in a given bargaining unit. The tools of coercion were theirs, and they were extensively used.[33a]

Beyond this roving commission for the national organizations, the Wagner Act of 1935 spelled out a stringent list of prohibitions on employers.[34] The enforcement of these privileges and restrictions was assigned to a new administrative agency, the National Labor Relations Board, which had two primary functions, one administrative, one judicial. To quickly develop labor's leverage on the economy, the Board administratively determined which union was to be the collective bargaining agent for what industrial bargaining units.[35] The independent or community union became branded as the tool of employers and effectively removed from the industrial scene.[36] The Board thereupon assumed, under the Act, the combined roles of complainant, judge, jury, and prosecutor to determine whether any violations of the code had been committed and how to punish the recalcitrant employer.[37] If an "unfair labor practice" were found to have been committed by the employer, the Board was authorized to issue an order comparable to a court decree, directing such corrective action as it saw fit. The original itemization of unfair labor practices by the employer included:[38]

(1) direct or indirect interference with employees' right to organize or to conduct, for mutual aid, any concerted activities (strikes, boycotts, slowdowns, picketing, meetings, proselyting, etc.);

(2) showing any approval or disapproval of any employee organization or assisting one union against another in any way;

(3) showing any bias relative to union status in treatment of prospective or actual employees;

(4) penalizing any employee for invoking Board action;

(5) refusing to "bargain" with a union about any condition of employment—(this, perhaps the most dangerous clause of all and highly controversial, is now broadly interpreted to outlaw any unilateral action by an employer even in the improvement of his production facilities or the subcontracting of work which can be more efficiently done elsewhere).

By the express language of the Act the "bargaining agent" is bequeathed exclusive monopoly power in dealing with the employer.[39] It is virtually a criminal act for an employer to take any action affecting working conditions, wages, hours, shifts, or staffing without prior consultation with the union.[39a] Only the agent union may speak for employees in the bargaining unit, regardless of their membership or non-membership in the union.[39b] If the union calls a strike because of an unfair labor practice, such as the employer's refusal to bargain over what the management might erroneously consider its own prerogatives, e.g., the installation of labor saving devices, not only is the union freed of any responsibility under a no-strike contract clause but the employer must keep the strikers on his payroll.[39c] The "right to strike", though ill-defined, is taken to mean not simply the right to quit work in unison but the right to stop others from working, to peacefully picket all the employer's operations, and to retain a vested interest in the jobs abandoned as well.[39d] An individual who quits his job because he believes his employer to be treating him unfairly has no such vested right. With rare exceptions only a union may exercise the right since what is protected is "concerted" action. Therefore the employee has job security only by remaining in the good graces of a recognized union. The union's exclusive privilege in achieving job security is of inestimable value in maintaining union discipline and in exercising economic leverage on a national scale over both the employer, who may lose heavily in a work stoppage while the union leadership actually has very little to lose, and over the employee, whose rights are derived through the union. The privilege applies not only to the strike but to any "concerted activity" decided upon by the union leadership, such as a refusal to handle certain work, to work at certain hours, or on certain days, to permit any changes in "work rules," to allow introduction of labor-saving devices, to permit relocation of operations, and similar tactics which help to consolidate the existing membership.

By contrast, in our wonderland of industrial relations, the government's policy is "do as I say, not as I do." The following clause of the Labor Management Relations Act abruptly forecloses for millions of civil service personnel the conventional "right to strike." [40]

> It shall be unlawful for any individual employed by the United States, or any agency thereof including wholly owned Government Corporations to participate in any strike. Any individual employed by the United States or by any such agency who strikes shall be immediately discharged from his employment and shall forfeit his civil service status, if any, and shall not be eligible for re-employment for three years by the United States or any such agency.

In the civilian economy, in economic strikes, e.g. for higher wages or fringe benefits, as distinguished from "unfair labor practice" strikes, retroactive pay rights are not protected by law although reinstatement rights are.[41] The economic strike becomes ineffective, therefore, if replacements can be hired on the open market; however an unfair labor practice can be conveniently employed as an occasion to gain economic benefits or, by coercion of concerted discipline, the union may be able to economically excommunicate the employer's whole operation. To bring pressure to raise wages or shorten hours or block discontinuance of jobs, the union must depend on its comprehensive discipline. It should be clear then, that the macroeconomic role of the union in our planned economy is to serve as an instrument through which there can be maintained sufficient discipline in the working forces throughout the whole industrial complex to enable them to extract their optimum share of the Gross National Product.

The popular assumption has been that the Taft-Hartley Act of 1947 and the Landrum-Griffin Act[42] of 1959 corrected the distorted features of the Wagner Act of 1935. Amendments were made which were helpful in restoring confidence to industry, but the fundamental privileges and immunities of organized labor actually were preserved in toto. The Taft-Hartley amendments to the Wagner Act[43] attempted to spell out a parallel list of unfair practices on the part of labor to balance those previously specified for management. Piecemeal amendment has proven ineffectual in many ways, however, and judicial interpretation has substantially vitiated much of what Senator Taft sought to achieve in his legislation. The featherbedding and secondary boycott provisions are illustrative of the gap between theory and practice.[43a] Minor modifications in union technique permit easy evasion of the intent of the law. The provision for judicial review of the activity of the National Labor Relations Board[44] still leaves the courts substantially pre-empted of original jurisdiction. Union responsibility undeniably has been greatly enhanced by the legal entity concept[44a] under which they may sue and be sued for breach of contract, but the finding of the Supreme Court that courts lack cognizance of arbitration proceedings has furnished an effective escape from this clause.[44b]

The effect of the Taft-Hartley Act has been to strengthen the *status quo;* new unions are harder to organize, but the established unions are more firmly established. Labor discipline has become tighter in the already highly concentrated industrial power centers, because, due to the seniority rules in nearly all contracts, entrenchment gets steadily deeper until, as in the railroads, only old age can reduce the rolls. The extensive government machinery for arbitration, mediation, and conciliation established in the Taft-Hartley Act[45] has reduced the frequency of work stoppages by facilitating adjudication of contract interpretation disputes, but the trend toward nationally centralized control of contract terms continues unabated. The prestige of national unions is closely tied to the size and consistency of their contract gains. The provisions for handling national emergency industrial disputes by an eighty day "cooling off" period[46] is a weak substitute for injunctive process against interference with individual freedom of choice. So long as our basic law tends to encourage tightly organized international and national unions with protected interests in abandoned jobs, there will be industry-wide bargaining or follow-the-leader bargaining. We shall be confronted with a most dangerous situation as long as a small handful of labor leaders is privileged to throw the country into economic paralysis. This is not a necessary adjunct to unionization.[46a]

To summarize the present legal status of unions in the national economy, they have been furnished the exclusive prerogatives to maintain very effective discipline not merely within their own ranks but throughout our industrial complex. This discipline is conducive to national rather than local organization. Immunity to laws against the restraint of trade and to conventional equity jurisdiction together with their special "bargaining agent" monopoly give the national union the tools to maintain tight discipline which in turn wields tremendous economic power.

Let us change our focus of interest from the area of macroeconomics, the national economic entity, to the area of microeconomics, the individual firm, community, or innocent bystander. The classic statement of current policy was set forth in the case of *Garner* v. *Teamsters Union* in 1953.[47] Here a small trucking firm in Pennsylvania had been subjected to a typical teamster "stranger" strike. There was no labor dispute between the firm and its twenty-four employees of whom only four were union members. The firm handled local intrastate deliveries and pickups for a railroad. Mr. Beck's international organization sought designation as "bargaining agent." It sent outsiders to picket all operations of the trucker. The trucker's business fell off 95% because no other drivers would cross the picket lines. The trucker, his business ruined, asked for an equitable injunction in the Pennsylvania state courts to halt the picketing since there was no majority of union men in his own organization and no dispute with his own employees. The lower court granted the injunction to thwart an obvious unfair labor practice. The Pennsylvania Supreme Court declared the injunction exceeded the State's powers. The case was appealed to the Supreme Court on the constitutional principle that private rights were enforceable at state law. Mr. Justice Jackson writing the affirming opinion said:[47a]

> Congress did not merely lay down a substantive rule of law to be enforced by any tribunal competent to apply the law generally to the parties. It went on to confide primary interpretation and application of its rules to a specific and specially constituted tribunal and prescribed a particular procedure for investigation, complaint and notice, and hearing and decision, including judicial relief pending final administrative order. Congress evidently considered that centralized administration of specially designed procedures was necessary to obtain uniform application of its substantive rules and to avoid these diversities and conflicts likely to result from a variety of local procedures and attitudes toward labor controversies.

> . . . This case would warrant little further discussion except for a persuasively presented argument that the National Labor Relations Board enforces only a public right on behalf of the public interest while state equity powers are invoked by a private party to protect a private right. . . . We conclude that when federal power constitutionally is exerted for the protection of public or private interests, or both, it becomes the supreme law of the land and cannot be curtailed, circumvented or extended by a state procedure merely because it will apply some doctrine of private right. To the extent that the private right is in conflict with the public one the former is superseded. . . . Of course Congress in enacting such legislation as we have here, can save alternative or supplemental state remedies by express terms or by some clear implication if it sees fit.

We cannot but wonder what might have been conceived to be the meaning of the Ninth and Tenth Amendments to the Constitution which read, "The enumeration in the Constitution, of certain rights, shall not be construed to deny or disparage others retained by the people." and, "The powers not delegated to the United States by the Constitution nor prohibited by it to the States are reserved to the States respectively or to the people." Presumably the Court concedes that Congress in its wisdom may place centralized economic control higher in our scale of values than abstract personal or community rights.

In 1895 when Eugene Victor Debs was challenging the authority of the courts to hold him for contempt in the continued violence of the Pullman strike, Justice Brewer in explaining the authority exercised said:[48]

> It is curious to note the fact that in a large proportion of the cases in respect to interstate commerce

> brought to this court, the question presented was of the validity of state legislation in its bearing upon interstate commerce. If a State with its recognized powers of sovereignty is impotent to obstruct interstate commerce can it be that any mere voluntary association of individuals within the limits of that State has a power which the State itself does not possess?

Today the answer to Justice Brewer's question is not as obvious as at the turn of the century. Confronted with challenging problems in industrial relations the injured party appears to have no alternatives under the present laws other than acceding to the union demands or passing the responsibility to the executive branch of the federal government. Celebrated recent episodes include the steel strike of 1959, the tugboat strike in New York harbor in January 1961, and the tie up of air traffic a month later. The final settlement in the 1959 industry-wide steel dispute was arranged only after the personal intervention of Vice President Nixon. Furious legal battles had ended in the application of the Taft-Hartley injunction after collective bargaining had proceeded fruitlessly for several months. In the settlement wages gained another lap on productivity. The price-profits squeeze became more intense. Markets for structural materials, lost to other producers, stayed lost, and the foreign trade balance remained badly distorted. One year later the tugboat crew dispute,[49] involving merely sixty-two jobs, forced President Kennedy to dispatch his Labor Secretary straight from the Inaugural to devise a deferral of the crucial featherbedding issue; 100,000 commuters to Manhattan had been stranded for a week and the strike, coupled with blizzards, had threatened the great metropolis with gradual starvation. Trains were halted from Cleveland to Providence. Less than a month later all civilian air traffic was shut down and 80,000 employees idled by a wildcat walkout of highly paid flight personnel in a jurisdictional dispute.[50] Again the President found it necessary to intercede and defer the issue by appointing a special *ad hoc* conciliatory body.[51] The dilemma has been created by excluding labor issues from federal courts on the grounds they are *not* commerce[51a] and from state courts on the ground of federal pre-emption under the National Labor Relations Act and the Railway Labor Act, which are predicated on the *conduct* of commerce!

State "right to work" laws and state court authority to award tort damages in certain labor cases or injunctions in certain obvious cases of impending or continuing violence are at best peripheral influences in the industrial relations field.[52] The sovereign constitutional authority of the State and of its component communities to act in either their own public interest, or on the behalf of injured citizens whose personal rights have been transgressed, has been so frequently countermanded in the field of labor disputes that that main element of order, prestige, and sovereign dignity has been effectively destroyed. Few intelligent persons will waste time attempting to get a local remedy when the odds clearly indicate the remedy will be overruled by exercise of the doctrine of federal pre-emption.[52a] Thus in the microeconomic sense there is little a community can do in self-defense. Union power is of a larger order than state sovereignty.

As to the capacity of employers to exercise effective bargaining power in their relations with union organizations under the present legal ground rules the following extract from a report of the Senate Committee on Labor and Public Welfare concerning the bill based on the McClellan investigations speaks for itself:[53]

> When it comes to immunities, business enterprises enjoy none while labor unions enjoy many. The latter are immune from the Federal income tax and similar taxes in a number of the States. Only employers pay the unemployment compensation tax, the railroad unemployment insurance tax, and the payments required under workmen's compensation laws by both Federal and State Governments. Unions are not subject to the Federal antitrust laws and have substantial immunity from the granting of injunctions against them by the Federal courts under the Norris-LaGuardia Act and in some States which have little Norris-LaGuardia Acts.
>
> Among the additional privileges and immunities enjoyed by labor unions are the following:
>
> 1) The Federal Government in the Taft-Hartley Act specifically guarantees them against interference with their internal affairs, nor are they required to be incorporated under either State or Federal law. Corporations on the other hand owe their existence to State corporation law and their activities are limited to the provisions of their corporate charters which are required to be in conformity with State law.
>
> 2) Labor unions have immunity against the misconduct of their members who are engaged in union activity as, for example, strikes and picketing. This kind of immunity is not possessed by other types of unincorporated associations.
>
> 3) Labor unions enjoy the right to bargain exclusively for all the employees in the unit, including those employees who are strongly opposed to the union. This can mean, as it often does, that a union selected as the bargaining agent by as few as twenty-

five percent of the employees in the unit becomes the bargaining spokesman for all the employees.

4) Labor unions are not subject to anything similar or equivalent to suits by minority corporate stockholders against their corporations.

5) Through collective bargaining contracts labor unions may require union membership as a condition of continued employment although employers are forbidden by law to require nonmembership in a union as a condition of employment.

6) Unions enjoy a right to strike without either the union or its members being penalized therefor. If the strike results from the employer's unfair labor practice, the strikers cannot be replaced. The employer does not have any equivalent right to engage in a lockout, except in two types of situations, both extremely rare and both of minor significance. All other types of lockout are illegal under the Taft-Hartley Act.

7) The prohibition imposed on unions by the Taft-Hartley Act against restraint and coercion of employees is limited to physical violence, direct economic coercion or to threats of either of these two types of conduct. On the other hand, the prohibition imposed on employers under the act is against interference as well as restraint and coercion which is forbidden to unions.

8) When management discriminates against an employee in violation of the Taft-Hartley Act, the Board may issue not only a cease-and-desist order but may require the employer to reinstate such employee and to pay him back pay as well. These remedies are in substance sufficient to take care of most of the unfair labor practices committed by employers and to restore employees to the status they would have enjoyed if the unfair labor practices had not been committed. Unions, on the other hand, even though they may engage in illegal conduct which results in loss of pay for employees, are not required to com-

pensate employees for such loss, except where the union itself was responsible for causing an employer to discriminate. Thus an illegal mass picket line where picketing denies access to the plant to employees who wish to continue to work and which as a result causes such employees to lose pay is not the type of misconduct which the NLRB has required the offending union to remedy by compensating the employees for loss of such pay, but an employer must compensate for loss of pay suffered by locked-out employees.

9) Unions have the right under certain circumstances to examine an employer's books and records in the course of collective bargaining. The employer has no equivalent right.

10) Labor unions in many situations have a legal right of access to the employer's property, the right to compel the employer to make his property available for use by the union, and the right to invade the privacy of employees who are not union members and sometimes even against their wishes. Employers enjoy no equivalent or similar rights.

If the public is relying on corporate management to balance union power, it is relying on a badly handicapped champion. Those who wonder what became of the "equal protection" clause in the Constitution must remember that it occurs in the Fourteenth Amendment which applies to the States and not to the federal government. The more uncharitable might say it was passed to humiliate the South and should not be taken out of context.

We come now to an area in which legal relationships begin to become quite tenuous. This is the area of intra-union and inter-union affairs. It has already been indicated that the union as an entity is much less distinct than the corporation. The union may officially act for many employees who are not members and it may have many members who are not employees of the bargaining units for which it is the official agent. In theory it is a voluntary non-profit unincorporated association and it historically has had great privacy, flexibility, and diversity internally. As anyone with any experience in purely voluntary organizations is keenly aware, their records, their financial dealings, and their adherence to any purportedly authentic by-laws or constitution, leave much to be desired. Members not part of the controlling group are usually powerless to make their opinions or interests felt in the administrative procedure, particularly if strong-willed or unscrupulous persons have acquired office. It is only natural if members and non-members are both represented by a bargaining agent that the non-members will suffer a comparative disadvantage. Further, as Bertrand Russell has pointed out,[54] "Love of power is very unevenly distributed. Those who most desire power are the most likely to acquire it. In a social system in which power is open to all, posts which confer power will be occupied by men who differ from the average in being exceptionally power loving." Human inertia makes unions undemocratic.

Understandably the governments both federal and state have been exceeding hesitant to project themselves into internal affairs of unions or any other voluntary associations. A concept of "freedom of association" has been virtually annexed to our Bill of Rights.[55] The First Amendment declares the "right of the people peaceably to assemble and to petition the government for a redress of grievances." The Railway Labor Act states among its purposes the intent "to provide for the complete independence of carriers and of employees in the matter of self organization."[56] The Norris-LaGuardia Act declares in its statement of the public policy of the United States ". . . though (the individual unorganized worker) should be free to decline to associate with his fellows, it is necessary that he have full freedom of association, self organization and designation of representatives of his own choosing, and that he shall be free from the interference, restraint or coercion of employers of labor . . ."[57] The National Labor Relations Act declares "Employees shall have the right to self-organization, to form, join or assist labor organizations . . . and to engage in other concerted activity . . . for mutual aid or protection."[58]

Clearly at the onset of modern labor legislation there was an intent simply to equate the employees' freedom of action in the forming of associations with the freedom of action of their already highly organized employers. Actually, the employers through the state corporation laws and through special federal regulatory legislation were already extensively regulated as to the form of their internal organization. Though the regulation of business enterprise has grown since by leaps and bounds, the first hesitant steps toward regulation of the internal affairs of labor by the federal government were taken in the Labor-Management Disclosure and Reporting (Landrum-Griffin) Act of 1959.

The events leading to the passage of this Act were authoritatively summarized in the Final Report of the Select Committee on Improper Activities in the Labor or Management Field, U. S. Senate 1960, popularly known as the report of the McClellan

Committee. The activities of this committee were a springboard for several important statesmen, including Senator John Fitzgerald Kennedy, his brother Chief Counsel Robert F. Kennedy, and Senator Barry Goldwater. The disclosures of the Committee centered around corruption in labor's officialdom, particularly the underworld typified at the infamous Appalachin conference muscling into legitimate business in the guise of organized labor; the collusion and bribery by which employers and labor officials exploited workers, notably in the Chicago area; the coercive activities of the Teamsters Union to destroy small enterprises, envelop unwilling employees, and misuse the vast financial resources of the union; and the large scale employment of coercion, open and covert, by the United Auto Workers in the Kohler strike in Wisconsin and in the Perfect Circle strike in Indiana.

The resultant legislation was a compromise which neither of the major protagonists, the labor and management lobbies, were happy about. Primarily the enactment sought to ensure a modicum of democracy in the unions. The method of accomplishing this objective was to promulgate for every union which sought, directly or indirectly, to function as a bargaining agent under the National Labor Relations Act, a set of minimum requirements as to: (a) the rights of its members to express ideas at variance with those of the union hierarchy;[59] (b) the reasonable control and publication of financial decisions and dealings of union officials;[60] (c) the conduct and frequency of elections;[61] (d) the private enforcement of members' rights in federal and state courts;[62] (e) the limitations of the trusteeship concept whereby national unions arbitrarily exercise control of the funds, voting power and operations of local unions;[63] (f) the screening and bonding of union officials with fiduciary responsibilities;[64] (g) the more specific prohibition of collusive practices between dishonest employers and labor officials;[65] (h) and by means of amendments to earlier legislation the distinct assurance that some judicial or quasi-judicial forum would be authorized to accept jurisdiction of each labor dispute.[66]

This legislation has not as yet been sufficiently digested by the judicial system to appraise its effectiveness. It marks a distinct retreat from the blanket immunity which unions enjoyed from internal regulation and the injunctive process. The authority of state courts as well as of federal courts is partially reasserted.[67] The administration of protective ground rules similar to those which states employ in regulating the internal affairs of corporations has been allocated to the Federal Department of Labor for all formally constituted labor organizations.[68] Many aspects of the law appear to require further clarification and particularization, but the primary theme appears to be further pre-emption by the federal government and greater centralization of authority, particularly in the Secretary of Labor, now an immensely powerful post.

From this analysis of the legal status of union power, successively from the aspects of macroeconomics and microeconomics, from the viewpoint of the management and of the wage earner, it should be evident that although the climate of the laws of employment has varied considerably over the last thirty years, the basic pattern has remained the same. The inviting mirage of countervailing economic power led us on and on into centralization of labor, of industry, and of government. But centralization has brought its own fearsome train of undesired side-effects. Democracy is no more sure in a national union than in a huge corporation. Government is not more benign because it is larger. Freedom in the sense of diversity of choice of employment for the worker and of economic alternatives for management has become substantially less. For the lobbyists and the propagandists the task has been made much simpler, for the responsibilities have been transferred to fewer and more pliable hands, further removed from public view. The relationship of cause and effect, and of incentive and impetus, has been increasingly beclouded. In a figurative sense the embrace of our society by the long arms of George Orwell's Big Brother has become a tight bear hug.[69]

FOOTNOTES — III

[1] See *U. S. Congressional Code and Administrative News* (1959), 2418.

[2] *Constitution of the United States, Analysis and Interpretation,* U. S. Government Printing Office, Washington, D. C., 1953, 686.

[2a] The clauses in note II—2 applied only to the States.

[3] The favorite citation is some dicta from the Philadelphia Cordwainers Case (1806), 3 Commons and Gilmore, *Documentary History of American Industrial Society,* 1910, 59, 233.

[4] See Frankfurter and Greene, *The Labor Injunction,* Macmillan Company, New York, 1930, 3 and notes.

[5] See Milton Handler, "Schoolmaster Case," (1411), 12; "Meat Market Case," (1433), 13; "Case of the Tailors of Ipswich," (1614), 32; "Case of Monopolies," (1602), 44, *Trade Regulation,* Foundation Press, 1960.

[6] See Letwin, "English Common Law Concerning Monopolies," 21 Univ. of Chicago Law Review, (1955), 355.

[7] Statute of Monopolies (1624) in the reign of James I.

[8] Edward S. Mason, Harvard University Press, 1959, 5.

[9] *Ibid.,* 25.

[10] See J. K. Galbraith, *American Capitalism — The Concept of Countervailing Power,* Houghton Mifflin Company, 1952.

[11] See particularly Section 9, National Labor Relations Act, 29 U. S. Code Sec. 159.

[12] See 49 Stat. 449, Act of 5 July, 1935, 29 U. S. Code Sec. 151, *et seq.*

[13] 47 Stat. 70, Act of 23 March, 1932, 29 U. S. Code Sec. 101-115.

[14] *Legislative History of the National Labor Relations Act, 1935,* Volume I, United States Government Printing Office, Washington, D. C., 1949, 15.

[15] 295 U. S. 495.

[16] 49 Stat. 449, 29 U. S. Code Sec. 151.

[17] 61 Stat. 136 (1947).

[18] Quoted in Livingston Shirt Corporation Case, 107 NLRB No. 109 (1953); also Hendrick, *Bulwark of the Republic,* Little Brown & Company, Boston, 1937, 425.

[19] 52 Stat. 1060, Act of 25 June, 1938, 29 U. S. Code Sec. 201-219.

[20] Social Security Act, 42 U. S. Code, Sec. 301, *et seq.*

[21] Employers Liability Act, 45 U. S. Code Sec. 51-60; Railroad Retirement Act, 45 U. S. Code Sec. 215, *et seq.*; Federal Insurance Contributions Act, 26 U. S. Code Sec. 1400, *et seq.*; Unemployment Compensation Act, 42 U. S. Code Sec. 501, *et seq.*

[22] 60 Stat. 237 (1946).

[23] 60 Stat. 23, as amended, 15 U. S. Code Sec. 1021.

[21] See NLRB v. Jones and Laughlin Steel Corp., 301 U. S. 1 (1937). This opinion by Chief Justice Hughes reversed 3 cases from different U. S. Circuit Courts of Appeal, challenging the powers of NLRB, each of which had come unanimously to an opposite conclusion. Perhaps no event since the Civil War has had greater long term impact on the subsequent political character of the United States.

[25] 328 U. S. 108 (1945) and 156 F. 2d 958 (1946).

[26] Southern United Ice Company v. Hendrix, 153 F. 2d 689 (1946).

[27] Farmers Reservoir and Irrigation Co. v. McComb, 337 U. S. 755 (1948).

[28] Lorain Journal Co. v. United States, 342 U. S. 222 (1951).

[29] See Sec. 14(c) of National Labor Relations Act, 29 U. S. Code Sec. 164(c).

[30] U. S. Code Congressional Service, 79th Congress, 2d Session, 1946, 1068.

[31] See generally: Slichter, Healy and Livernash, *The Impact of Collective Bargaining on Management,* Brookings Institute, Washington, 1961, and Bradley, *The Public Stake in Union Power,* University of Virginia Press, Charlottesville, 1959.

[32] See Sylvester Petro, *Power Unlimited,* Ronald Press Company, New York, 1959.

[33] Sec. 13 of Norris-LaGuardia Act, 29 U. S. Code Sec. 113, and United States v. Hutcheson, 312 U. S. 219 (1940).

[33a] The classic example of this is the Apex Hosiery Case, Apex Hosiery v. Leader, 310 U. S. 469 (1940); see also NLRB v. International Rice Milling, 341 U. S. 665 (1951).

[34] Sec. 8(a) of National Labor Relations Act, 29 U. S. Code Sec. 158.

[35] *Ibid.,* Sec. 159.

[36] See Senate Report 105, 80th Congress, 1st Sess. 12-13, and International Association of Machinists v. NLRB, 311 U. S. 72 (1940).

[37] Sec. 10 and 11, National Labor Relations Act, 29 U. S. Code Sec. 160, 161.

[38] Sec. 8(a) of National Labor Relations Act, 29 U. S. Code Sec. 158.

[39] *Ibid.,* Sec. 159.

[39a] NLRB v. J. H. Allison Company, 165 F. 2d 766 (1948).

[39b] Matter of National Tube, 76 NLRB 1199 (1948).

[39c] See NLRB v. Lion Oil Company, 352 U. S. 282 (1957).

[39d] NLRB v. Business Machine and Office Appliance Mechanics, 228 F. 2d 553 (1955).

[40] 61 Stat. 136, see particularly Sec. 305 of Statute, 129 U. S. Code Sec. 141-197.

[41] NLRB v. Remington Rand, 94 F. 2d 862 (1938).

[42] 73 Stat. 519.

[43] These clauses although enacted in Taft-Hartley are in the form of amendments to the Wagner Act and are found now as parts of 8(b) therein.

[43a] See 39(d) above and 10 *Labor Law Journal* 175 (1959) as to boycotts; as to featherbedding, 345 U. S. 100 and 345 U. S. 117 (1953); the make-work problem under the Railway Labor Act is even more troublesome.

[44] Sec. 10(f) National Labor Relations Act, 29 U. S. Code Sec. 160(f).

[44a] Sec. 301 Labor-Management Relations Act.

[44b] 80 S. Ct. 1358, 1343, 1347 (1960), also see Paul R. Hays, "Supreme Court and Labor Law, October Term, 1959," 60 *Columbia Law Review*, 901, 919-935 particularly.

[45] Sec. 202 Labor Management Relations Act establishes the Federal Mediation and Conciliation Service.

[46] *Ibid.*, Sec. 206-210.

[46a] Art. I, Sec. 10, U. S. Constitution forbids any state entering an alliance or confederation. Sherman and Clayton Acts control corporate combinations. That we should countenance in labor what neither government nor industry is permitted speaks more clearly than words the power of unions.

[47] 346 U. S. 485 (1953).

[47a] *Ibid.*, 490.

[48] In re Debs, 158 U. S. 564 (1895).

[49] For a thrilling blow-by-blow account of this comic-opera type affair involving the employment of one extra deckhand on each of nine ferry boats and fifty-one tugboats, see front page of the *New York Times*, January 20 to January 31, 1961.

[50] See News item in the *New York Times*, February 18, 1961, 1, col. 1.

[51] *Ibid.*, February 24, 1969, 1, col. 8.

[51a] Sec. 6, Clayton Act, 29 U. S. Code Sec. 17: see also sec. V below, 10-12.

[52] See Arnold Schlossberg, "Current Trends in Labor Law in Virginia," 42 *Virginia Law Review* 691, particularly 701 *et seq.* (1956).

[52a] Amalgamated Association etc., v. Wisconsin Employment Relations Board, 340 U. S. 383 (1958); see generally Albion G. Taylor, *Labor and the Supreme Court*, 2nd edition, Braun Brumfield, Ann Arbor, Michigan, 1961, 167-185.

[53] *Legislative History of Labor-Management Reporting and Disclosure Act of 1959*, Vol. I Office of General Counsel, NLRB, 511-512.

[54] *Power*, W. W. Norton Company, New York, 1938, 14-15.

[55] See U. S. v. Cruikshank, 92 U. S. 542 (1876) and Hague v. Committee for Industrial Organization, 307 U. S. 496 (1939).

[56] 45 U. S. Code Sec. 153.

[57] 29 U. S. Code Sec. 102.

[58] *Ibid.*, Sec. 157.

[59] 73 Stat. 519, Sec. 101 (a), (1) and (2).

[60] *Ibid*, Sec. 201.

[61] *Ibid.*, Sec. 401.

[62] *Ibid.*, Sec. 102 and 103.

[63] *Ibid.*, Sec. 301 to 305.

[64] *Ibid.*, Sec. 501-504.

[65] *Ibid.*, Sec. 202 and 203, and Sec. 302 Labor Management Relations Act.

[66] Sec. 14(c), (1) and (2), National Labor Relations Act, 29 U. S. Code 164 (c), (1) and (2).

[67] Labor Management Reporting and Disclosure Act, Sec. 102, 603, 609, 610.

[68] *Ibid.*, Sec. 607, 610.

[69] George Orwell, *Nineteen Eighty-Four*, Harcourt, Brace & Company, New York, 1949.

Good laws lead to the making of better ones; bad ones bring in worse.

J.-J. ROUSSEAU: The Social Contract, III

IV.

SOCIAL INCENTIVES AND ECONOMIC EFFECTS OF UNION POWER

Since 1930 Americans have painfully acquired a maturity and a broadened view of the challenge of industrial relations which they lacked when our basic labor legislation was formulated. Archibald Cox, reflecting a sadder but wiser general opinion of our labor movement, recently commented as to its results:[1]

> The most important qualities cannot be instilled by legislation or judicial decision. The law cannot compel members to assert their rights. It cannot teach them to view their unions as something more than service organizations hired to obtain benefits in return for dues. It cannot create the spirit of self-government or restore a sense of mission. The future of the labor movement probably depends less upon the course of legal developments than upon its capacity to feel and express the highest ideals of the community.

The purpose of this section is to attempt a brief analysis and evaluation of the reasons for the absence of the "sense of mission" and "capacity to express the ideals of the community" which dismay so keen an observer as Cox.

Jefferson declared it self-evident that man's Creator had endowed each citizen with an inalienable right to the pursuit of happiness.[2] Such pursuit implies a distinct plan of effort or work on the part of each individual, for happiness is a most elusive condition. Von Mises suggests a greater refinement of man's immediate motivation than pursuit of that uncertain happiness which so many fail to recognize on sight.[3] He points out that man may work or strive to train his mind and body for future tasks; he may work to satisfy a religious, charitable or selfless compulsion; he may work to divert his thoughts from less pleasant things or to avoid boredom; but most frequently he works because the compensation offered him for working is more attractive than the enjoyment of idleness. The fundamental impetus in any group or society derives from the incentives motivating the individuals comprising it. Beyond the mere animal instincts of hunger, want of companionship, and want of comfort, these incentives spring from man's spirit, that divine spark, deeper within than conscious intellect, which inspires in each individual the whole long series of decisions made in the pursuit of happiness.

Our most celebrated study in motivational research, the Bible, tells us that man does not live by bread alone.[3a] Economic and non-economic objectives constantly compete for man's will and interest. How then should be decided the occasion and purpose of his strivings?

The essence of the concept of a free society is that each of its members must make such decisions uncoerced. Each decision boils down to a choice as to when to work or to loaf and what to work for when working. This choice is called liberty. It is an ideal long sought but never completely attained throughout any of man's societies. Those who seek this ideal were once called liberals. Nowadays there appears confusion as to whether the goal of individual freedom of choice continues to be the meaning of modern liberalism.

Regardless of the true nature of liberal aims, as our society approaches that economic millenium which Franklin Roosevelt felicitously described as "freedom from want", non-economic motivations assume greater importance to the working man. Also as the millenium approaches in which economic purposes become secondary, the sociologists become more agitated about the absence in our society of the sense of mission which cannot be developed by legislation. Where indeed is the wellspring of that sense?

Von Mises describes the nature of society as:[4]

> ... concerted action, cooperation ... the outcome of conscious and purposeful behavior. The actions which have brought about social cooperation and daily bring it about anew do not aim at anything else than cooperation ... with others for the attainment of definite singular ends. The total complex of the mutual relations created by such concerted actions is called society. It substitutes collaboration for the isolated life of individuals. Society is the division of labor and the combination of labor. ... The individual acts and lives within society. But society is nothing but the combination of individuals for cooperative effort.

Those who fail to concede that individual freedom of choice is the well-spring of our society's sense of mission he analyses in this manner:[5]

> Universalism and collectivism are by necessity systems of theocratic government. The common characteristic of all their varieties is that they postulate the existence of a superhuman entity which the individuals are bound to obey. What differentiates them one from another is only the appellation they give to

> this entity and the content of the laws they proclaim in its name. The dictatorial rule of a minority cannot find any legitimation other than the appeal to an alleged mandate obtained from a superhuman absolute authority. . . . It does not matter whether the absolute ruler bases his claims on the divine rights of anointed kings or on the historical mission of the vanguard of the proletariat. . . . The priests of this creed ascribe to their idol all those attributes which theologians ascribe to God—omnipotence, omniscience, infinite goodness and so on. If society or state is an entity endowed with all the qualities ascribed to it by collectivist doctrine then it is simply nonsensical to set the shabby individual's trivial aims against its lofty designs.

Toynbee finds a religious note in Communism[6] but theocracy in its conventional sense is no longer to us the issue it was to Jefferson. It has been transmuted into a form of nationalism which seeks to clothe the central government with ultimate powers in all things. Our chief juristic defense against this authoritarianism has lain not so much in freedom of religion as in the Fifth and Fourteenth Amendment phrase "nor shall any person be deprived of life, liberty or property without due process of law."

The substitution in the Bill of Rights of the word "property" for Jefferson's "pursuit of happiness" in the Declaration deserves comment. Property is a word of many meanings. The common connotation of wealth is scarcely adequate. Perhaps individuality is the closest approximation. Property may be "corporeal or incorporeal, tangible or intangible, visible or invisible, real or personal."[7] Legally a man's property comprises those relationships over which he may by law exercise the power of decision.

Without property rights man's liberty is meaningless. He has property in that over which he may exercise, at law, a degree of control. The very definition of constitutional government places the wellspring of decision in our economy in the will of its members. The whole purpose of a constitution is the limitation of the sovereign power to the determined will of its citizens. From them has the authority issued. Under our constitutional concept each citizen retains both a right and presumptive ability to dispose of or exchange his property as he sees fit and to align himself freely with such social endeavors or societies as his personal motivation might incline him. His government was designed to assure him these rights and not to make such decisions for him. The distinct delineation of this relationship was the primary purpose of the Bill of Rights.

As the agricultural communities of Jefferson's day shrank relatively to an ever smaller segment of our federal society, relatively fewer citizens retained substantial economic independence from the vicissitudes of commerce. A nation of self-employed became largely wage earners. The self-confidence which had stemmed from wresting one's own living from the forest or the soil or from independent practice of an acknowledged skill steadily dwindled as that living came to depend largely on the whimsy of a foreman, the kindliness of an employer, or the success of an enterprise in which the wage earner had neither a significant responsibility nor a channel of communication. As industrial employment became largely impersonal and virtual industrial armies were first recruited during the nineteenth century the old trade or craft union filled an important social need which previously had been of minor consequence in the economy, namely the maintenance of morale, a feeling of confidence and power of decision based on mutual economic support.

The more zealous labor theorists were early swept away with enthusiasm for the martial potential of industrial armies. Cox states:[8]

> According to one view labor unions should be regarded as military organizations for their function is to wage economic warfare with employers who are constantly feeling out chinks in the union's defenses through which to wound if not destroy them. As a wartime army can neither brook divided leadership nor tolerate active dissidents so must a union punish the troublemakers in order to close ranks against employers and rival organizations.

Our labor movement maintained conservative aspirations as compared with corresponding social endeavors elsewhere. Receptive to the wisdom of Smith and Jefferson, we became heirs to an unusually flexible political economy in which power was widely diffused. As a result, the type of labor radicalism which turned Germany to National Socialism, Spain to Syndicalism, Italy to Fascism and Russia to Bolshevism never gained control here. Not even did we go so far as the British and Australian labor movements carried those sister states. The pragmatism of Samuel Gompers overcame the emotionalism of Eugene Debs, and the American Federation of Labor with its autonomous locals held firmly together where the Knights of Labor with their more grandiose social and political ambitions disintegrated. The Industrial Workers of the World achieved lasting infamy for their intransigence whereas the Railway Brotherhoods cautiously salvaged some valuable prerogatives from the fiasco of the Pullman and Shopmen's strikes. The selfish particularism of practical labor leaders like John L. Lewis, Harry Bridges, and James Hoffa paid big wage dividends to their supporters, whereas the more outright political radicals like William Z. Foster and Henry Wallace have wasted their supporters' substance on vain forays which only accentuated the internal divisions in the labor movement.

The trade union could claim the wholehearted devotion of its members in the days when they had no other means but mutual assistance for the achievement of their urgent economic ends: the maintenance of the knowledge of certain useful crafts, reasonably safe and decent working conditions, adequate income to advance the standard of living of the worker's family, assurance of a reasonable degree of job security, and the dignity of status or standing in the community. Today unions, national in scope and determined to overcome individualism, are more impersonal than management. Government agencies have taken over many chores the unions once attempted. The art of personnel management has recovered considerable lost ground for employers. The current spiritual lassitude of the labor union movement in this country is a symptom of economic progress. When we observe the havoc caused by overzealous labor leadership elsewhere we should be most thankful that this is so. It is impossible to analyze the social aspirations of organized labor without simultaneously considering the state of its economic well being. Man's cupidity is a sizeable factor in his activity, but the intensity of his will to cooperate with any given social movement will surely subside as its focus of interest begins to bore him or its accomplishments cease to be essential to him.

Our citizens are now, more than ever before, subject to a great diversity of influences, each urging or offering its own social objectives and an opportunity for individual cooperation. Competing societies in bewildering profusion focus their interest variously in religion, sport, business, art, politics, charity, education, hobbies or military activity. Each offers fellowship, diversion, and exhilaration of a physical or spiritual nature in varying degree. As the average work week has diminished in length, as our communications systems have improved, and as the adequacy of our economic well-being has advanced, the importance to the individual of social endeavors outside the mainstream of the economy has obviously correspondingly increased. The progressive feature of our federal tax structure has tended to discourage individuals from a greater commitment to purely economic ends than necessary to satisfy average wants. The punitive income tax, unemployment compensation, and social security appear to have significantly diminished the desire to work for compensation, the economic impetus of the average citizen. Employment taxes and the minimum wage laws have diminished the desire of employers to offer compensation. Regardless of the soundness of Professor Galbraith's economic theory as set forth in his best selling treatise *The Affluent Society*[9] it is quite evident from our climbing debt curves that his notion of our arrival in the Promised Land was in tune with the outlook of the contemporary generation.

By our own constitutional definition[10] the purpose of society in the United States is simply the

STATISTICAL DATA AS TO WAGES & CORPORATE INCOME IN THE UNITED STATES: 1934 - 1959

INDUSTRY	Avg. Hourly $ Wage	Corporate Gross Income in Millions	Net Income in Millions	% Profit before tax	Avg. Hourly $ Wage	Corporate Gross Income in Millions	Net Income in Millions	% Profit before tax	Avg. Hourly $ Wage	Corporate Gross Income in Millions	Net Income in Millions	% Profit before tax	Avg. Hourly $ Wage
	1934	1939	1939	1939	1939	1950	1950	1950	1950	1959	1959	1959	1959
Bituminous Coal	.72	817	−6	−1	.90	2420	163	7.0	2.00	2040	47	2.3	3.19
Railroad Transportation	NA	4754	36	1	NA	10690	1341	12.5	1.55	11370	464	4.1	2.58
Motor Vehicle Production	.72	3668	366	10	.93	18733	3296	17.5	1.73	19873	1085	5.5	2.67
Electrical Equipment	.61	1867	179	10	.74	10612	1417	13.3	1.45	19973	1276	6.4	2.21
Textile Materials	.48	3895	151	4	.47	13176	1240	9.4	1.20	12105	412	3.4	1.57
Rubber Products	.47	1084	63	6	.77	4055	435	10.6	1.57	6980	421	6.0	2.46
Steel Production	.63	2687	92	4	.85	11424	1521	13.3	1.66	1425	1276	9.0	3.08
Manufacturing Total Avg.	.55				.65				1.45				2.22

Note: The data as to wages has been obtained from the monthly Labor Reports of the Department of Labor. The data as to the corporate income comes from the annual reports of the Bureau of Internal Revenue, "Analysis of Corporation Returns."

cumulative will of its members. The trade union movement when it was yet a purely voluntary endeavor, unconfused by government intervention, chose to focus its attention not on class struggle or political ambitions but on economic improvement, on the solid Scotch rationale that many a mickle makes a muckle. This approach has gone about as far as it can go. Unionism's main concern now is to hold its relative position of dominance. Bearing this responsibility blunts its earlier social aspirations.

At this point let us digress from sociological aspects of the labor movement in order to examine some economic data which state the same story in a different way. The statistics in the attached table have been gleaned from the reports of the Bureau of Internal Revenue and from the monthly Labor Reports of the Department of Labor. They illustrate that in the twenty-five years from 1934 to 1959 the median increase in hourly wages of typical unionized labor in this country has been in the order of 300%; coal miners wages rose from $.72 to $3.19, auto workers from $.72 to $2.67, electrical workers from $.61 to $2.22, steel workers from $.63 to $3.08. The overall manufacturing average rose from $.55 per hour to $2.22 per hour. At the same time the *per capita* disposable income for the nation as a whole increased from $411 in 1934 to $1,906 in 1959, an even greater rise than in the hourly rates in the unionized industries. When converted to real buying power the *per capita* income of 1959 actually represents only about twice that of the 1934 income.[11]

It should be noted that labor's gain in the unionized industries over the last quarter century is not a relative one compared to that of the population as a whole. Organized industrial labor has gained more in income than have unorganized labor, those engaged in agriculture, or the pensioners. A great increase of income has occurred among the self-employed, the federal civil service and the supervisory groups. Inflation's toll is greatest among those whose incomes are not subject to frequent adjustment. It is an interesting but inconclusive academic exercise in economics to attempt to determine the extent to which the increase in labor income carries the national economy with it, as the Keynesians theorized, or the extent to which the acceleration of the latter carried the labor income upward, in the classical tradition. It is clear that as labor becomes more expensive the premium placed on labor saving devices becomes greater, i.e., the marginal utility of machinery increases. The most drastic overall reduction in the labor force, however, has occurred in agriculture, a non-union field. There also the productivity has increased the most on a *per capita* basis. The labor force in agriculture has declined from ten million in 1934 to five million in 1959. Meantime the ranks of unemployed fell from about twelve million to around four million, from 22% to 6% of the work force. The vast reduction in numbers in the agricultural work force and in the unemployed have tended to magnify the apparent gain in the nation's *per capita* income over the span of years we are examining, since the negligible earnings of these groups in 1934 lowered the average initial earnings figure well below the current wage of the employed industrial worker. As the investment in industrial development abroad begins to reach a level comparable to ours on a *per capita* basis, and as their markets broaden to a comparable volume of consumption, our ability to maintain the present wage disparity will end. Our growing "hard core" unemployment problems today reflect the squeeze between our arbitrary minimum wage and the broadening pressure of foreign competition.

Since 1934 farm income has risen from five billion to twenty billion dollars. Corporate profits, after taxes, have catapulted from one to twenty-three billion. The government's tax take from corporate income has increased even more sharply and defense expenditures have risen from less than one-half billion per annum to a rate of forty billion dollars. The total national income has risen tenfold, from fifty to five-hundred billion in nominal dollars. Consumer credit has increased from four to fifty-two billion and the national debt has increased from twenty-eight to two-hundred and ninety billion. Obviously this kind of acceleration cannot continue without inflationary disaster.

These comparative statistics have been cited to illustrate the fundamental and drastic change which has taken place in the national economy since the basic union immunities were enacted into federal legislation. We have witnessed a phenomenal re-orientation in our economic circumstances. In 1934 continuing deflation and economic stagnation discouraged investment and new enterprise to an alarming degree. Today continuing inflation and consequent over-anticipation of income have become of primary economic concern. No mere change of phase in the national economic cycle is behind this, but a world-wide industrial, social, and political upheaval in which the whole order of magnitude of the galaxy of national economies is changing. In the turbulent last quarter century the increase in wage rates in our areas of major industrial concentration, where unionization ratios are high, has widely outstripped gains in productivity, thus creating an increasingly artificial market condition.[12] Our consequent increasing difficulty with competition from abroad has caused the desire to control inflation to become a major influence in international as well as in national policy.

Statistics do not reveal another major economic consideration which has grown up in the interim. This is the problem of accelerated industrial innovation and obsolescence; the ever more rapid introduction of new products, new processes, and new distributive techniques. There is no statistical comparison which can adequately express the difference between 1934 and today in the scope of technological research, scientific production management, product development, and mass marketing.[13] These factors are placing a premium on the flexibility of our work force and of our invested capital which makes their capacity for rapid redeployment of fundamental importance to our role as a world power. Factors which tend to impede this redeployment of either work force or plant investment threaten dire consequences to the overall success of the economy. Reactionary labor forces today repeatedly deny to industry the freedom to adopt laborsaving innovations or to reap the fruits of technical advance. Unions with a vested interest in inefficiency, demanding continuation of unnecessary jobs and wasteful practices, are perhaps the greatest internal obstacle to the growth of the economy.[14] It is a paradox that these forces and their allies can mask themselves with the cloak of "liberalism."

To find the sense of mission which activates the composite will of the working man or of the union member, it is clear that we must look beyond economics. The will of the union member is surprisingly consistent with that of the surrounding climate of public opinion. A recent survey by the Opinion Research Corporation of Princeton, New Jersey has shown that 60% of union members favor closer regulation of unions by the government, as compared with 67% of the general public.[15] Fifty-seven percent of the union members believe laws against monopolies should apply to unions, as compared with 62% of the general public. Government appointed boards to investigate facts and recommend settlements in case of strikes were favored by 84% of the union members and 77% of the general public. Union membership is not the dominant characteristic of our wage earning citizens. To find the source of their animation we must look to the ideals and objectives of the whole of our society. American society is notoriously fluid, not stratified. The mechanism we have for advancing the purposes of that society is a fairly admirable device as such things go. It is called the federal republic; the unions in reality are a subordinate grouping in a most complex assembly, lower than states and communities in the proper order of priority. It is trite to say that we should give greater weight to the public interest than to any special interest, but the patent fact is that we are not doing so in our economic planning.

The functions of the unions in this country, according to Cox are: (1) to substitute group economic power for individual weakness in determining conditions of employment; (2) job security;

(3) to establish a rule of law in industrial relations; and (4) to enable workers to participate in industrial policy making.[16]

Each of these four roles appears to be falling increasingly into the penumbra of governmental responsibility under social legislation. Although the unions represent only 30% of the non-agricultural work force, the labor union lobbies have been virtually the sole voice of labor in agitation for this legislation. To induce favorable governmental action, strong leverage on the mass media of communication is needed. Therefore it would seem necessary to add to the functions listed above a more important fifth, the design and conduct of an effective public relations campaign on behalf of wage earners.

The climate of public opinion is the primary concern today for many in the top hierarchy of labor unions. Indeed much of the time it would appear that the officers of national organizations have little else to concern themselves with, since the day-to-day relationship with the employer is the function of the local. The national or international unit has no regular business to run beyond investing its funds and sponsoring its own expansion. It does not buy and sell nor produce, nor conduct any research worthy of the name. Its leaders do, however, increasingly give their attention not merely to the persuasion of Senators, Congressmen, State officials, and administrative agencies, but also, from their elegant marble and glass headquarters around Capitol Hill they patronize the columnists, the editors, the writers for magazines, stage and screen, and the visiting international political figures. Thus is maintained not only good will through a broad spectrum of communication channels but also a meaningful prestige, a public luminosity for labor leadership. The Orientals call this "face" and they wisely set great store by it.

Edward H. Chamberlin, Professor of Political Economy at Harvard, states that of over six-hundred million dollars in dues collected by our labor unions in 1957, about 60% went to local treasuries and 40% to the international organizations.[17] Undoubtedly some of this is for necessary salaries and strike "war chests", but a sizeable amount of the 40% is available for and employed in the public relations field. We cannot help wondering what a good cost analysis of the functions Mr. Cox spells out would show as against the expenditures made for purposes he does not itemize.

It is difficult to survey industrial relations in the United States without concurring in the general attitude of the union members that their unions are primarily service organizations hired to obtain benefits in return for dues. They compete for the public ear and the legislative assist along with the Chamber of Commerce, the American Legion, the National Education Association, the American Medical Association, and the National Association for the Advancement of Colored People, to mention only a few. The labor movement in this country has had repeated opportunities to go off on a wild goose chase similar to those which have enthralled the more imaginative and ambitious labor leadership abroad where the social structure was less fluid and accordingly more conducive to collectivist aberrations. Despite temptations this has not occurred. One significant reason why is that Americans are by heritage a very restless people, infrequently given to prolonged dedication to any cause. This restlessness or inconstancy is virtually all we had in common to begin with. It is what brought most of our progenitors out of the old world and into the new. Our physical perambulations, our job turnover rate, and our wholesale shifts of population have been on a scale utterly without parallel elsewhere. Our communications systems are more universal and more completely permeate the whole of our society. Foreign observers accustomed to more variegated and static societies consistently remark on the pervasive homogeneity and sameness they find here. These circumstances have produced among us the closest approximation to that perfect information dissemination system considered necessary to the economists' model of perfect competition.

Union members are typical conscientious citizens motivated by a sense of mission consistent with the rest of our society. They can perceive what the market price for various skills is and where the markets are, and they move accordingly. But there are many considerations which move them other than the market price for labor: the dignity of the work, the security of the industry, the congeniality of surroundings, the availability of satisfactory living and recreation facilities, the proximity of kinsmen, the promise of future advancement, and climate are but a few of the obvious considerations which the individual worker takes into account if he is not in dire economic distress. These choices are not potentially within the scope of union control other than, to a slight degree, the first two. Accordingly our work force is "atomized," whether the economic planners like it or not. The individual must continue in large measure to decide his own employment, and our government has in the Employment Act dedicated itself to the proposition that he should have an election in making a decision. The hiring halls of the National Maritime Union, the shape up of the International Longshoremen and the orchestral assignments of the Musicians Union are anachronisms, despite a recent Supreme Court decision sustaining them under current legislation.[18] These devices are poorly suited to the individuality of the American worker. The unions which insist upon them are fighting in retreat and against the economic tide.

Let us agree, then, that the union is a boon to the worker in aiding him to obtain a reasonable degree of job security and fair administration of work assignments and work rules. To a degree it can assist in keeping his wage scale in phase with the national prosperity. So far as the union does substantially assist in attaining these objectives and also in keeping an edge in wordwise with the legislative committees and the mass communications media, it well deserves the support of working men. It is something entirely different, however, to say that these functions demand the extension of privilege in the form of monopoly power over industrial communities, or broadscale control of the national supply of personal services in a given field of industry. Such power is clearly a serious interference to the proper allocation of resources through the open market.

Some monopolies undoubtedly are essential. For example much of the national defense must remain a government monopoly. Our public utilities, transportation and communications systems are also essential monopolies. Although largely in private management, they must remain under strict government regulation as to rates and services rendered. Our patent, copyright, and trademark laws all grant limited monopolies in the use of various inventions, compositions, and devices in order to stimulate and reward the very important ingenuity of the more enterprising elements of our society.

Our society demands, in the case of any monopoly, that the public interest retain either direct control or strict regulation. The Sherman, Clayton, and Federal Trade Commission Acts[19] were designed to supplement the common law and state statutes to prevent abuses by private monopolies and restraints of trade. A great body of state and federal legislation and regulation for the same purpose has followed in the same vein, establishing regulatory agencies designed to manage indirectly those private enterprises which, for economic reasons, must be allocated a degree of monopoly power. The government directly manages other vital enterprises such as the production of materials for nuclear fission or fusion.

The primary balance of our economy is obtained through the competitive market. The allocation of resources in realty, in facilities, in manpower and in materials is governed in this country, and ultimately in the western sector of the international economy, by the law of supply and demand which von Mises calls the consumers' sovereignty.[20] To the extent that there is an asserted purpose backed by purchasing power, an equivalent effort will be expended in the economy to supply that purpose. This is the economic freedom, the diffused power of decision, which Adam Smith expounded. To fully establish the alternative, a controlled economy, we must abandon the principle of the consumers' choice, give up the objective of a free society and relinquish our fundamental political and social beliefs. Economic well-being is not an end in itself, however. It is merely ancillary to the enhanced development of individual talents. Neither economic well-being nor individual freedom is advanced by granting special immunities and privileges to an unnecessary monopoly.

To illustrate the point let us examine two current and cogent examples of the effect of special privilege. In San Francisco harbor, as result of monopoly power used efficiently and unsparingly on the waterfront, the International Longshoremen's and Warehousemen's Union recently wrung out of the local steamship and stevedoring employers, the Pacific Maritime Association, a five year contract which provides that the employers will contribute five million dollars per year above and beyond very liberal pay and fringe benefits, for the "privilege" of introducing labor saving devices and methods into cargo handling.[21] The money is to accrue in a trust fund to the benefit of the longshoremen who lose their jobs as result of the introduction of such devices. Among the features involved are palletized loads which can be swung directly on to vehicles without any additional handling. Immediately upon the effectuation of this agreement and introduction of the labor-saving devices the Teamsters Union went on strike and picketed the docks because their work had been reduced by the palletized loading scheme decided on by the employers and the longshoremen's union.[22] The Teamsters had not been consulted. This, they maintain, constitutes an unfair labor practice on the part of management. After a complete dock tie-up of four days the employers agreed to suspend the use of labor-saving methods pending decision in court or before the NLRB. Meantime the hush money continues to have to be paid to the Longshoreman's Trust Fund at a rate of over $12,000 per day. The aggrieved employers have brought suit in the District Court for triple damages against the Teamsters Union under clause 301 of the Labor Management Relations Act, and under the Sherman and Clayton Acts.[23] Judgment is pending, but a favorable decision is unlikely because the pre-emptive clauses of the Wagner Act give the NRLB exclusive jurisdiction over this commerce, the Clayton Act says labor is not commerce, the Norris-LaGuardia Act denies the court authority in a labor dispute to enter a restraining order, and the National Labor Relations Act guarantees the union a right to concerted action. Thus is justice bound hand and foot.

Our railroads in the last ten years have converted at great expense to diesel operations. Billions of dollars have been expended to replace locomotives, to modify repair equipment and fuel facilities, and to retrain personnel. One of the advantages of the shift was that fewer men would be needed to operate the trains. Before the shift tremendous sums had had to be paid by the railroads to the coal companies and on to the United Mine Workers' welfare fund to appease them for the prospective reduction in mine employment. After the shift the Railroad Brotherhoods through threat of strike refused to allow the reduction of train crew personnel to be effected. A Royal Commission in Canada after reviewing the same problem two years ago ordered the crews reduced on Canadian trains. A special investigating commission appointed by President

Eisenhower two years ago is still "studying" the matter here. The cost of the delay is estimated at $500,000,000 per annum to the railroad owners and the shippers, but the public will pay in the end. The wheels of progress are braked in the Railway Labor Act perhaps even more effectively[24] than under the National Labor Relations Act.

These incidents illustrate perhaps the most pernicious feature of our substantive labor legislation and its most serious interference with the economy. This is the misconception, stemming from the mandate to "bargain," that management has an obligation to take no action affecting working conditions without union approval. The growth in the economy lies in increased productivity, which today depends on an increased plant investment per working man in each industry. The doctrine of federal pre-emption, together with union immunity to injunction, make the courts powerless to offer a remedy when progress is wilfully obstructed. If management is denied the prerogative of improving its plant and its efficiency because the unions choose to force the retention of stagnant work rules, we have little but defeat to look forward to in the cold war.

Those who would believe that the Taft-Hartley Act effectively outlaws featherbedding as an unfair labor practice and prevents such goings-on, are invited to read the classic case of American Newspaper Publishers Association v. National Labor Relations Board.[25] In this case the practice of the International Typographical Union, requiring newspaper publishers to pay for setting bogus type for the advertisements which were actually reproduced from a cardboard mat, was challenged and brought to the

Supreme Court on *certiorari.* The undisputed fact is that the bogus type is immediately destroyed after being set and serves absolutely no purpose other than to get more pay for the union members. The court ruled, however, that the practice was acceptable since "work", wanted or not, was actually being done and therefore the pay for doing it did not fall under the Taft-Hartley prohibition of "an exaction for services not performed or not to be performed."[26] That a local union should attempt to achieve job security by such devices is understandable, but that such stupidity should be countenanced as the intent of national economic policy is preposterous.

Economics is the science of allocation of goods and resources to meet the requirements of a given society or economic unit. The economy of our society is necessarily based on free enterprise rather than state socialism. The principles of free enterprise are intimately interwoven with the concept of political liberty. The free market is one which anyone so desiring is at liberty to enter as a buyer or a seller, be it services or commodities. Such a market is governed by the natural laws of economics rather than the artificial restraints of politics. But the pretense of open competition is patently false when the allocation of the most vital element in the economy, employment or labor, depending on your perspective, is largely controlled by a privileged monopoly or cartel. With competition hobbled it becomes impossible to achieve a satisfactory allocation of goods and resources unless there is put into effect some comprehensive plan of arbitrary distribution, the political routine of ever greater taxing and spending, which becomes, finally, expropriation and redistribution. Wittingly or unwittingly the sector of our national economy governed by arbitrary political expropriation and redistribution is now steadily eclipsing the once open market governed by competitive principles.

Our post-war administrations have been forced to accelerate the pace of expansion of governmental responsibility at the federal level because of the severe artificial restrictions in the mobility of labor and in the freedom of action allowed employers under our employment statutes. The net effect of our labor monopolies is that workers are unable to move freely into the highly compensated fields where demand exceeds supply and industry has been increasingly inhibited from moving into areas where labor is in ample supply and living costs are low.

To illustrate, if carpenters and pipefitters were paid up to $600 per week at missile sites it was because of the throttle-hold of union monopoly on such services. Thousands of patriotic workers, ready, willing and able to furnish equivalent services for more reasonable wages obviously were artificially restricted from competing. Meantime the Federal government, as customer, made the sky the limit by giving *carte blanche* to contractors to pay, on a cost reimbursement basis, whatever was necessary to get the job done under such handicaps.

We can no more blame the unions for getting the best they can for their members than we can blame the auctioneer who gets the best price he can for his seller and so sells to the highest bidder. We can only blame ourselves for our negligence in letting the market be so easily rigged against the public interest. As they say in the Law, he who sleeps on his rights has no complaint. The logical economic correction is to rescind the special privileges of the monopolists, but the probable political correction will be another commission, division or bureau which will employ an assorted collection of experts in labor relations, statistics, economics, data processing, program planning, etc. These honorable servants will make a whale of a project out of their undertaking. Later, as the dust of confusion rises and as the access to the elementary facts becomes utterly impenetrable, some practical determinations will be made and a compromise will be reached whereby a basic wage of $450 a week will be established plus $150 in fringe benefits. In return the union hierarchy will probably agree not to publicly oppose the administration's program. Such is the standard operating procedure for any good, self-maintaining bureaucracy. The easy answer is simply to leave things as they are so long as an electorate comprised of the progeny of Barnum's customers is sucker enough to keep on paying the bills.

FOOTNOTES — IV

[1] *Law and the National Labor Policy,* University of California, 1960, 111.

[2] *The Declaration of Independence* (1776), second sentence.

[3] *Human Action, A Treatise on Economics,* Yale University Press, 1949, 584 *et seq.*

[3a] Deuteronomy 8:3.

[4] *Human Action, op. cit.,* 143.

[5] *Human Action, op. cit.,* 150.

[6] See generally *Christianity Among the Religions of the World,* Charles Scribner's Sons, New York, 1957, particularly 14, 17, 18.

[7] See Black's *Law Dictionary,* 4th edition, 1382.

[8] See *Law and the National Labor Policy, op. cit.,* 93.

[9] *The Affluent Society,* Houghton Mifflin, Boston, 1958.

[10] Preamble, *Constitution of the United States* (1787).

[11] See generally George L. Bach, *Economics,* Prentiss-Hall, 1958 Chap. 7, 117 *et seq.*

[12] See generally Slichter, Healy and Livernash, *The Impact of Collective Bargaining on Management,* Brookings Institution, 1961.

[13] See generally John Chamberlain, *The Roots of Capitalism,* Van Nostrand Company, 1959, particularly Chap. 9.

[14] See Morris A. Horowitz "Featherbedding, the Specter in Future Collective Bargaining," 11 *Labor Law Journal* 19, (1960).

[15] See study entitled "Forces Shaping the Decline of Labor Union Power," *15th Trend Study on National Labor Issues,* Princeton, New Jersey, August 1960.

[16] See Harrington and Jacobs, *Labor in a Free Society,* University of California, 1959, 45, 46.

[17] "Labor Unions and Public Policy," *American Enterprise Association,* 1958, 2.

[18] Carpenters Local 60 v. NLRB, 42 *Labor Cases,* 16887; NLRB v. Hod Carriers Local 324, 38 *Labor Cases,* 65769. These citations are 1961, from Commerce Clearing House.

[19] 15 U. S. Code Sec. 1-7, 12-27, 49-51, respectively.

[20] *Human Action, op. cit.,* 270-272.

[21] See "Memorandum of Agreement on Mechanization and Modernization" dated 18 October, 1960, signed by J. Paul St. Sure for Pacific Maritime Association and H. R. B. (Bridges) for International Longshoreman's and Warehouseman's Union.

[22] See *San Francisco Examiner,* March 8 and March 10, 1961, 1.

[23] See "Automation Deal", article in *Business Week,* March 25, 1961.

[24] See Sec. 2 of Railway Labor Act "General Duties". The sixth, seventh, ninth and tenth articles when combined make it virtually

impossible to change the archaic *status quo* without litigation and red tape which continues for years at great expense to the carriers.

[25] 345 U. S. 100 (1953); a comparable case in the entertainment field is NLRB v. Gamble Enterprises, 345 U. S. 117 decided the same day.

[26] Sec. 8(b), (6) National Labor Relations Act as Amended.

Power feeds on its spoils, and dies when its victims refuse to be despoiled. They can't persuade it to death; they can't vote it to death; they can't shoot it to death; but they can always starve it to death.

BENJAMIN R. TUCKER: Instead of a Book, 1893

V.
THE PRIORITY OF STRUCTURE AND PROCEDURE

In the preceding sections we undertook to trace historically the growth of union power within the framework of our federal system, to analyze the factors which made it the darling of the Law, to appraise the social aspirations which first animated labor organizations and the changes therein which have since evolved. We noted finally the elementary theory upon which the economy of a free society operates and the incompatibility therewith of monopoly power in any forms other than those strictly limited or regulated in behalf of the public interest. We confront now the dilemma of corrective action; how to maintain effective morale among our wage earners and proportionate economic growth throughout the whole of our society without such an over-centralization of authority as to throttle the individual incentives necessary to keep us abreast of our competitors in the international economy. What alternatives are open to us? Of these, which offer the surest and most practicable long-term solution amid the extremely complex and delicate system of social, economic, and political relationships which must be adjusted to any change?

A perceptive student of law, government, or economics cannot examine the heterogeneous superstructure which federal statutes and rulings dealing with the regulation of industry and of employment have erected atop our basic legal system without recognizing that an unmanageable task has been created for those charged with the administration of justice, as well as for those charged with responsibility for the economy. It is impossible for the judiciary, with its present truncated authority in the field of industrial relations, to interpret any consistent intent of the law as to the rights of individuals or the priorities of various aspects of the public interest, from statutes based on such diverse social objectives and economic theories as motivated the authors of the Bill of Rights, the Sherman Act, the Wagner Act, the Employment Act, and the Reporting and Disclosure Act.

The statute books are cluttered with anachronisms. The need for separate procedures for industrial relations in rail and air transport, as distinguished from trucking and maritime transport or the rest of industry, has evaporated with the broadening of the "commerce" concept. The extent of federal intervention throughout the field of industrial relations is today so great that the proscriptions of the Norris-LaGuardia Act in its present form are antediluvian. The administrative enforcement features[1] of the Wagner Act no longer have any proper place in the system. It is inconsistent and illogical for the National Labor Relations Board to stand as a permanent judicial body in addition to its important administrative responsibilities.

For the economic planners it is sheer chaos to attempt simultaneously to implement the policy line of the Employment Act, to maintain a specified "growth" rate, to encourage our necessary foreign alliances, and to acquiesce in continuous political distortion of our economy by such "gimmicks" as arbitrarily accelerated minimum wages and tenaciously retained "make-work" practices which price our products and services out of the market and thus actually render a steadily larger number of persons unemployable.

One thing seems clear: the whole economy cannot be efficiently planned unless it be wholly controlled. It cannot be wholly controlled with any serious pretense of a free society. Something has to give.

The Anglo-American concept of justice cannot be molded into an economic flywheel. The settlement of disputes is a problem apart from economic progress. A distinct portion of the responsibility for our economic decisions must be removed from federal regulatory agencies and restored to the hands of our individual citizens and of our component communities. The determination of personal rights in employment disputes is a job which must be restored to the judiciary. Our basic plan allocating responsibility for economic decisions[2] was unceremoniously abandoned a generation ago due to great pressure from those who favored security over freedom. The judiciary was forced to waive decisional responsibility as to torts and contracts concerning labor and to cede authority to a central bureaucracy whenever the bureaucrats chose to intervene. Today perhaps we should take a greater pride in the burdens of a free society.

Proponents of the labor monopoly remain obsessed with the concept of countervailing power.[3] Proponents of corporate empire confound size with efficiency. Groping for security in a changing economy they grasp at merger and diversification to float on the tide of inflation. The tax policy of the federal government continues to reward complacency and penalize innovation, prod consolidations and discourage new entrants into the economy.[4] The regulatory agencies continue to grow more steadily than the economy. Multiplying pressure groups accelerate their agitation in a treadmill pursuit of comparative governmental favor. Our states and communities stand largely muted, hamstrung by pre-emption and frustrated by confusion throughout the whole area of economic policy. Big corporations beget bigger labor organizations. Together they have made necessary still bigger and more inaccessible government. It is essential for us to re-emphasize that these institutions are the servants, not the masters, of our society and its component communities. The hour is late; the situation far gone to the limits of retrieve.

Before assaying to recommend any specific courses of corrective action let us consider two premises of fact, one concerning the nature of collective bargaining, one concerning the nature of unions today.

Collective bargaining is here to stay. The impersonal relationships of our vast industrial corporations have submerged the individuality of wage earners who not only have learned that they have no bargaining power standing alone but have found that the circle of minor supervisors with whom each must deal has little or no control of working conditions. To lay hand on the principals it is necessary to "pierce the corporate veil." On paper, management comprises the officers of corporations and the supervisors in their plants. Actually these are mostly hirelings, like the wage earners themselves. Somewhere behind the corporate veil lurks a controlling interest that actually designates the directors, hires the officers, and guides the policy. This is the real interest which must be brought into the light at the bargaining table to make an enforceable contract.

Let us dismiss from controversy, therefore, any question of the need for a master contract defining basic conditions of employment. At the same time it is most essential that we not confuse the master contract with the specific implied or expressed job-order-level agreements with individual parties.[5] Both levels of the contract exist; both are important, and we shall do well to distinguish between them.

Unions actually do not contract to supply the labor necessary on a job. They are incapable, as bargaining agents, of assuming responsibility in the event that their members or the parties whom they represent quit their work without just cause. Clearly there actually must exist in any industrial operation employing labor an express or implied contract between the employer and each individual employee, whether or not there is a collective agreement between a bargaining agent and the employer. Where there is a collective agreement, there are many unanswered questions as to how it is incorporated in, or pre-empts, the individual contracts. The use of master contracts, under which a series of specific job orders are required for work to be undertaken, is a fairly simple and widely used contracting device which appears a sound analogy for treating the relationship between collective agreements and individual contracts of employment. There is no good reason for treating industrial employment as independent of the established field of contract law which became integrated into the common law over two hundred years ago.

Traditionally the administration of contract law has been subject to the substantive law of the States. It has been developed primarily in state legislation and state courts. Federal courts taking cognizance of contract controversies between parties of diverse state citizenship apply state law using federal procedures.[6] Recently the doctrine has been set forth in Supreme Court decisions to the effect that the collective bargaining agreements, being an object of special solicitude under our federal labor law, must be governed by a new body of federal substantive law to be developed by arbitration rather than state or federal courts or legislation.[7] This view is illustrative of the paralyzing economic uncertainty generated by the constantly changing purposes and allocations of responsibility in our federal system under our collectively incoherent federal statutes in the field of industrial relations.[8]

Let us summarize our first premise in this manner: the principle of collective bargaining is a fundamental legal technique in an industrial economy, but it falls within the conventional pattern of contract law, and it underlies or complements rather than pre-empts individual contracts for rendering services in exchange for compensation.

The second essential premise before proceeding to corrective action is recognition that unions are now amenable to damage suits in ways not anticipated thirty years ago. Once the equitable injunction was virtually the sole remedy of any efficacy in industrial relations. It was frequently used because damages as distinguished from equitable remedies, were ineffectual. Unions in their role as bargaining agents now have acquired a legal entity and sizeable property[9] which can be reached by judgments placing upon them the liability for tort, breach of contract, or statutory violation.

The basic criteria for a satisfactory resolution of the challenge of industrial relations, beyond a clear view of the facts, are two: first, individual freedom of choice should be reinforced, not only that of the worker but also that of the consumer and that of the innovator and entrepreneur; second, the basic defenses and traditional remedies of Anglo-American jurisprudence should be restored to the parties affected by the dispute. Prior distortions for partisan advantage adopted during an emergency urgently require correction. The strained structure of our federal republic must be shored up if it is to carry the ever increasing responsibility we have assumed in world affairs. Our central administrative machinery has long since been swamped with extraneous chores it was never designed to handle.

It is the main contention of this paper that the desirable fruits of the American labor movement can best be preserved by the consistent application of the concept of separation of powers.[10] The prescription here offered to overcome the obvious imbalance in our political economy is structural and procedural rather than substantive in nature. We must put first things first. Recognizing the transient nature of substantive law as compared with the permanent character of federal structure, it is essential to revive the concepts of dual sovereignty and continuing segregation of executive, legislative, and judicial functions. In the field of economic regulation these elementary principles have been forgotten or have become hopelessly confused.

The inescapable first step in correcting the evils besetting us in the field of industrial relations is to restore to the judiciary its peculiar judicial function. This involves a major reorientation of the provisions of the Norris-LaGuardia Act, and the restoration to the judiciary of those judicial functions lodged in the National Labor Relations Board by the National Labor Relations Act.

The second step is to recognize the necessity of observing another fundamental constitutional safeguard to our freedom, the doctrine of reserved powers[11] as expressed in the Bill of Rights.[12] This involves a clear and consistent delineation of the extent of federal authority under the pervasive commerce clause so that the States and their component communities may exercise some semblance of self-government in the field of industrial relations. The doctrine of federal pre-emption is proper and necessary in its sphere, but it has distinct limits, and the limits must be defined in fundamental law rather than left to momentary whimsy.[13]

The third and last step is to confine to principals rather than to intermediaries such privileges and immunities as are found necessary to be spelled out in the field of industrial relations. Individual citizens should be able to claim their rights directly through the courts without dependence upon the beneficence or cooperative humor of a union or arbitrator or satellite executive agency. The quasi-public functions of unions properly end upon completion of negotiations for the master contract. After the master contract is made, the individual worker should be able to assert his personal contract rights through a chosen counsel and forum without being beholden to anyone. He cannot properly enforce his rights today because he lacks access to a proper forum and independent counsel and has no standing within the scope of arbitration procedure.

As we have noted in the previous sections, the corporation preceded the union as a device for special privilege. The unmonitored development of the corporation as a private organization to advance industrial objectives led to such transgressions of the public interest that a reluctant Congress was forced to enact special restrictive legislation to protect the consumers from greedy men controlling dangerous concentrations of economic power. The travesties of corporations against their employees spurred the growth of unions and industrial violence. This struggle became a serious handicap to the nation's social and economic equilibrium. The sense of justice then prevailing in public opinion demanded some reinforcement of union prerogatives to enable the individual worker to cope with the corporation. Predicated upon the doctrine of countervailing power the Norris-LaGuardia Act was passed in 1932 applicable to all labor disputes, both in and out of the transportation field. It was followed three years later by the first version of the National Labor Relations Act which was confined to the "commerce" area not covered by the Railway Labor Act. The dislocation of the judicial functions in the field of employment torts and contracts stems from these three pieces of legislation. Let us examine the rationale of this legislation with the foregoing corrective formula in mind.

The first of these laws was a purely negative act. It severely restricted the authority of federal courts in controversies involving in any way the concerted activity of industrial workers. Perhaps the most lucid explanation of the need for this legislation as well as the most influential tract in its support was a book published in 1930 entitled *The Labor Injunction*[14] by Felix Frankfurter and his collaborator, Nathan Greene. Justice Frankfurter was then a well-known and respected Professor of Law at Harvard. His brief for the anti-injunction legislation proceeded on the reasoning summarized below.

The employment by federal courts of interlocutory injunctions, based merely upon affidavits to the effect that grave injury threatened the complainant, furnished a too convenient tool with which employers could paralyze union attempts to win recognition or economic concessions by strikes, boycotts, or picketing. Frankfurter analyzed all of the 118 reported federal labor cases involving injunctive relief in the period 1901 to 1928. He estimated an equal or greater number of unreported federal cases had occurred in which labor injunctions had been applied for. Some of these he also analyzed. His complaints were that the complete absence of federal law in the industrial relations field left the unions at the mercy of personal whim of individual judges; that the affidavits procedure was unreliable; that dangerously ambiguous and unsupported blanket edicts were commonly issued unjustly; that the advisability of accepting federal jurisdiction was questionable; that the transient nature of union enthusiasm was such that the injunction, though intended merely to freeze the *status quo* pending further investigation, actually could not achieve static balance in a dynamic situation and so in effect denied to the workers the right of concerted action. Further, he found that the absence of a jury trial in contempt cases made the authority of judges, unrestrained by special legislation, an arbitrary and tyrannous imposition on the right of unions to self-help in industrial disputes.

Most of the industrial violence up to that period had attended the organizational phase of labor activity since the counter-tactic of employers had been to nip unionization in the bud by refusing to recognize or deal with unions and by employing vigorous self-help measures of their own, such as strike breakers, private detective organizations, labor spies, and "yellow dog" contracts. Thus many of the big employers, running operations such as the railroads, the steel mills, the coal mines, and the automobile factories then appeared able to remain beyond the reach of unionization. In prescribing a cure for this situation Professor Frankfurter examined certain alternatives proposed. Said he:[15]

> Congress may withdraw the whole federal jurisdiction based on diversity of citizenship of the parties. Through claims of such diversity perhaps two thirds of the labor cases now find their way to the federal courts. Congress may repeal or modify antitrust laws or . . . repeal the provision of the Clayton Act granting private parties injunctive relief against violations of the antitrust law. But both these modes of reform would reach far beyond the domain of labor injunctions. A third method is to deal explicitly with labor disputes by defining and limiting the exercise of federal jurisdiction in such controversies. This mode of approach merely recognizes that industrial relations present distinctive problems for the wise use of judicial power.

The first two alternatives stirred too broad an opposition, and, although seriously considered by Congress,[16] were withdrawn in favor of the tailored immunity.

With this insight into the reasons for special immunity of unions from conventional equity jurisdiction let these observations be made:

1) The then existing vacuum of labor legislation and precedent, which Frankfurter found to be the real problem underlying the federal court's dilemma,[17] has long since been amply filled. Subsequent

federal laws and rulings have spelled out profusely the rights of labor organizations. The principle of federal pre-emption coupled with a very loose interpretation of the constitutional ambit of "commerce" has made state law of minor consequence in the matter of industrial relations.[18] As industrial activity has spread across the whole country, a formidable library of purely administrative law has been developed in interpretation of the federal statutes. Hence Frankfurter's complaint about the unpreparedness and lack of guidance in the federal judiciary has become distinctly outdated. Where the Norris-LaGuardia Act contemplated substantial withdrawal of federal jurisdiction, subsequent developments were exactly opposite.

2) No longer can we be swayed by the plea that special aid is needed because weak and transient labor organizations, too impecunious to sustain proper litigation for their rights, are easily shattered in morale by the psychological impact of a single injunction. We are dealing instead with an efficiently organized, well-financed, broadly based, and highly articulate special interest with tremendous political leverage, capable of seriously embarrassing the sovereignty of the federal republic itself.[19]

3) There are sound grounds for a critical review of the injunctive powers of federal courts. As long ago as 1912 John W. Davis, later Democratic presidential candidate, then a House member from West Virginia, singled out as he argued for the Clayton Act:[20]

> . . . at least five glaring abuses (of the injunctive power of the federal courts) which have crept into the administration of this (equitable) remedy: . . . the issuance of injunctions without notice; the issu-

ance of injunctions without bond; the issuance of injunctions without detail; the issuance of injunctions without parties; and in trade disputes particularly, the issuance of injunctions against certain well established and indispensable rights.

If it is necessary to curb the injunctive authority of the courts, the curb should be a general one along these lines, applicable to all classes of cases and should not constitute merely a special privilege for union labor. Recent blanket restrictions placed on State officials and legislators in school desegregation cases,[21] for example, set a precedent with ominous implications as to our basic prerogatives of self government. Surely the denial of jury trial for those held in contempt is as dubious a procedure against a critical legislator as against a labor agitator.

When the Norris-LaGuardia Act was under consideration the volume of reported labor injunction cases was perhaps ten to twenty *per annum* in federal courts,[22] many in the field of railroad operations, whereas the number of controversies presented to one of the substituted tribunals, the National Labor Relations Board, now runs in excess of twenty thousand per year.[23] Each of these cases is determined by a dismissal or a "cease and desist" order, the equivalent of an injunction, somewhat watered down in finality.[24] It should be noted that a substantial number of additional controversies are handled under the National Mediation Board and the National Railroad Adjustment Board, mechanisms of the Railway Labor Act.[25] Obviously we have now recorded for posterity that indispensable experience which, as Justice Holmes remarked, is the life of the Law, whereas it was not available in the field in 1930 when Frankfurter's brief was prepared.

A reappraisal of the whole field of legislation touching on union power is presently in progress in the Senate Committee headed by Senator McClellan. The Committee has sought the advice not only of labor relations experts but also among men of overall comprehension in the Law, leading advocates, judges of the courts of highest appeal in industrial states, and professors of Law in leading law schools.[26] Clearly the Anti-injunction Act cannot be considered independently. Although it was written when the statute books were virtually blank, today continued supplementary legislation and shelves of reported case law virtually engulf the original act. Therefore let us more closely examine the relationship of Norris-LaGuardia to the National Labor Relations Act and the Railway Labor Act in their current form.

The first nine sections of the National Labor Relations Act deal with findings and policies, definitions, the establishment of the National Labor Relations Board, the rights of employees, the itemization of unfair labor practices, and the method of designation of bargaining agents.[27] Essentially these sections provide the ground rules for the conduct of collective bargaining in that segment of the economy "affecting commerce" but not rail or air transport which are provided for separately. The tenth and eleventh sections of the Act, entitled "Prevention of Unfair Labor Practices" and "Investigatory Powers," bequeath exclusive and comprehensive judicial powers on the Board in the area of industrial relations, and give it the authority to:

> . . . issue and cause to be served on such person [as it has found to have been engaged in an unfair labor practice] an order requiring such person to cease and

desist from such unfair labor practice and to take such affirmative action, including reinstatement of employees with or without back pay, as will effectuate the purposes of this Act.

If the party on whom the "cease and desist" order is served fails to obey, the Board then is empowered to petition the Circuit Court for an injunction to enforce its order. By such time it would appear that the Norris-LaGuardia obstacles to the Court's authority to enjoin what it is that the Board has found "unfair" had been dissolved and that an injunction might issue if the court found the Board's contention valid and its order appropriate. In the rail and air industries the Adjustment Board operates on a similar basis.[28]

This centralized administrative procedure may have been necessary in the early days of large scale federal intervention in the industrial relations field where the whole concept of governmental participation in industrial disputes was novel, but today it is an obstruction to justice. Union organization is no longer delicate and has not needed the protection of a forcing frame for a long time. Litigants aggrieved by unfair labor practices are in the same shoes as those suffering any other tort. They should have immediate access to a court of original jurisdiction without prior intervention by an administrative body appointed on a political basis for a brief period, authorized to write its own rules, define its own jurisdiction, and prosecute its own case before itself as judge. The net result of such administrative technique after a score or more of years is best expressed in Eugene Rostow's characterization of regulatory bodies in general:[29]

> Many of the rules echo forgotten battles and guard against dangers which no longer exist. They comprise vast codes understood only by a jealous priesthood which protects these swamps and thickets from all prying eyes. The basic theme in the reform . . . should be to release the regulated industries as fully as circumstances permit.

As an alternative to lodging judicial functions in the NLRB a procedure parallel to that prescribed in the Bankruptcy Act[30] should be considered whereby there would be designated an officer of each of the federal District Courts comparable to the present Referee in Bankruptcy. This officer would be designated a Referee in Labor Relations. Similarly he would derive his authority from the District Court and within its jurisdiction have summary powers to hear complaints and to settle issues arising under those sections of the National Labor Relations Act or the Railway Labor Act dealing with the employee's rights or unfair labor practices. As in the case of the Bankruptcy Act, the summary authority of the Referee would be subject to the review of the court and the right of the litigants to demand a plenary session. Any employee, employer, union, or other party aggrieved by an unfair labor practice, a denial of statutory or constitutional rights, or by a breach of contract should be able to bring his complaint to be heard in a judicial climate in the same manner as any other civil action. The whole Wagner concept of having the government prosecute recalcitrant employers before a kangaroo court simultaneously exercising powers as complainant, prosecutor, judge and jury, should be junked as unworthy of a free people.

As at common law individual parties may contract to arbitrate their contractual misunderstandings. Arbitration can take a great load off the courts and deserves continued encouragement. The rapid increase in recent years in the volume of labor arbitration testifies to its comparative advantages. However, the subordinate status of arbitration to the judiciary must be maintained.[31] The courts must retain authority to review arbitration awards upon appeal and to grant a hearing to any party aggrieved. Certainly parties not personally signatory to a contract clause requiring arbitration deserve a right to a day in court.

The recision of sections ten and eleven of the National Labor Relations Act would substantially eliminate the explicit declaration of the doctrine of federal pre-emption in the field of industrial relations. To clarify the implicit doctrine, however, it is imperative that there be formulated an authoritative definition of what constitutes "commerce" in the sense it is used in Article I, Section 8, Clause 3 of the Constitution. The term is vaguely and differently defined at present in numerous related statutes.[32] It constitutes a vitally important definition of jurisdiction which cannot be slurred over. Too long have federal agencies been permitted to play fast and loose with the reserved powers of the States and of the people.

The present dichotomy as to the meaning of "commerce" borders on the absurd. The Clayton Act states flatly that the labor of a human being is not an article of commerce. The intent of the clause was to exclude labor from the jurisdiction of federal courts. The Norris-LaGuardia Act was written to *reinforce* this Clayton Act exclusion. The Wagner Act three years later glibly assigned virtually complete jurisdiction over industrial relations to the administrative board it created to effect its purpose, using the commerce clause as justification. Obviously if labor is not commerce, the federal government has no authority constitutionally for the labor legislation; if labor is commerce, antitrust laws cannot fairly except labor combinations from prosecution. The present double standard makes a mockery of the language of the Constitution.

If the "several States" have become an anachronism, a Constitutional Convention should be promptly convened to rewrite the Constitution wiping out such archaic references. Certainly the doctrine of dual sovereignty and reserved powers should not be allowed to bleed to extinction merely through the careless delegation of congressional authority to "regulate commerce among the several States."

The steady disintegration of self-government in our communities, if allowed to continue, will be disastrous to our freedom. While we agitate disruptively for self-government in the Congo, in Algeria, and in Angola, we suppress and pre-empt it in our component states whose traditions antedate the federal union. We ignore the possibility of extending our federal concept to other nations of common heritage, but constantly complain about the steady growth of the Soviet satellite system. The reconstitution of the dignity and authority of local and state governments in the field of industrial relations is essential not only to our political safety but also to the diverse and healthy economy visualized as an objective in the Employment Act.[33] In barring our component communities from self-government in the economic field we are cultivating an irresponsibility which will choke out the principle of limited government.

The economies of nations such as Sweden and Switzerland, though based upon substantially smaller resources and fewer people than many of our states, have nevertheless achieved in recent decades fuller employment, a more stable economy, and more peaceful industrial relations than we. Each of them emphasizes the voluntary nature of unionism.[34] Their ratio of unionization is much higher. So it is not truthful or in accord with the facts to label as anti-union a move to encourage voluntarism and autonomy. Each of our states, as a community, is not only capable of self-government but is more capable of efficient local economic management than are federal civil servants to whom authority has been delegated. To them, standardization for the sake of standardization has become a fetish and a convenient excuse for self-aggrandizement. Until Franklin Roosevelt raised the great furore over the resistance which the Supreme Court offered to his recovery program,[35] the original meaning of "Commerce among the several states," was expounded consistently by our judiciary.[36] Since 1937, when the court packing plan was defeated, there has been no limitation on the improvised interpretations of interstate "commerce."[37] If we are to retain the federal concept, in any real sense, either an Amendment or a policy promulgation by Congress, in the vein of the Employment Act supported by the Executive, is essential to define the scope of federal economic legislation. The Court, of itself, was unable to hold its position after the 1936 election.

An accurate definition of the original meaning

might be stipulated by Congress, as a preamble to a revised and consolidated labor code, thus:[38]

> The Congress declares that it is the continuing policy of the federal government, incumbent upon all officers of the United States, to interpret the power of the Congress, under the third clause of section 8 of Article I of the Constitution, to extend to the regulation of all exchanges of goods, documents, services, or rights in property, involving a diversity in citizenship between the parties to the exchange, and to all physical movement of goods, documents, or parties in the process of rendering service or transferring property rights, across the boundaries of the several states or territories of the United States in connection with any such exchange. The regulation of exchanges not directly involving any diversity of citizenship, nor any physical movement across the boundaries of the several states of the United States, of goods, documents, or parties in the process of rendering services or transferring property rights, is declared a power reserved exclusively to the jurisdiction of the state within which the exchange is conducted.

In the probably protracted interim until justice in the field of industrial relations is restored to a true constitutional equilibrium, it would be a great boon to the long suffering public to add a basic provision to substantive labor law. The core of substantive labor law now lies in the definition of "unfair labor practices" which are proscribed in the National Labor Relations Act. These provisions presently focus their attention exclusively on the interests of the union versus the employer. At present there are defined therein no practices which are unfair from the standpoint of the interests of the public, that is, the interests of members of the ambient community upon whom the industrial warfare tactics of behemoth labor factions and corporate enterprise must necessarily impinge. Short of the National Emergency provisions of the Taft-Hartley Act, which are only temporary expedients at best, the warring factions in our economy today can play havoc with the welfare of the hapless community at the site of battle without compromise of their exclusive privilege of "concerted action". The author contends that the injured third parties should have access to injunctive process via Federal and State Courts as an essential right of self-defense against abuse of the "concerted action" privilege of labor unions.

We already have available in the Antitrust Laws and the Federal Trade Commission, as earlier discussed, a right of action in the public and in the injured third parties against the aggressions of propertied interests. For the non-combatants no corresponding avenue of correction for the abuses of "concerted action" by labor unions is presently available. To remedy this deficiency an additional "unfair labor practice" should be spelled out in the National Labor Relations Act in this vein:

> It shall be an unfair labor practice for a labor organization, without lawful purpose and preponderant justification, to interfere with, restrain or attempt to coerce the activities of persons not in privity with the union, nor with the employer directly involved in the labor dispute, so as to damage them in the normal pursuit of their livelihood, or to interfere with the maintenance of their health and property, or to interrupt the conduct of their necessary travel in connection therewith. An adequate remedy for violation of this article may be sought by any party aggrieved through its violation, including a state or any of its agents, upon petition in any court of the United States exercising jurisdiction over the offending party.

Thus a cause of action and a forum would be afforded those third parties and the public who are presently without a remedy whenever corporate management and the labor cartel lock horns and trample on innocent bystanders. The special privilege of "concerted action" should be withdrawn from those who employ it to interfere with the necessary and lawful economic activity of their host community merely to bring indirect pressure on an industrial antagonist.

It is difficult for an objective observer surveying the field of federal industrial and social legislation to identify any sound reason why, in the quest for job security, we have diverged from the basic policy of individual rights established in the Federal Employers Liability Act,[39] the Jones Act,[40] the Longshoreman and Harbor Workers Act,[41] and the Unemployment Compensation Act.[42] In each of the latter cases an employee has a direct right of action. It is in no way contingent upon the existence of "concerted activity," of a certified bargaining agent, nor of the concurrence of a union. If it be necessary to the economy to protect job security as an element of national policy, the vested right to a job should be enforceable by the individual rather than by an intermediary whose interests may be substantially different and who may or may not be the selected counselor of the plaintiff.

This peculiar circuity of action has introduced the primary leverage of union power over the individual rights of their members. Unions represent less than a third of the non-agricultural work force. If job security is essential to our national economy, it should not be a special privilege for a small minority who use it primarily to gain relative advantage. The plaintiff in labor relations should be the principal and not the agent. He should have the privilege of selecting his forum in a state or federal court or before an arbitrator.[43] These prerogatives are extended to the individual worker in other social legislation. It is inexcusable that union power should have prevailed to acquire a monopoly in the matter of job security and working conditions.

In proselyting for additional members, in influencing public opinion, and in the employment of economic coercion, unions properly are acting in their own behalf as voluntary associations and deserve equal rights as such before the bar of justice. No public responsibility attaches to these latter functions and neither should there attach any special privilege or federal intervention. Only as a bargaining agent for an unwilling minority does the union assume a public responsibility, and only here is special privilege appropriate. The effective surveillance of this function is the true and proper responsibility of the National Labor Relations Board. In the interest of consistency the functions of the Board in this area should be extended to cover the air transport and rail industries which are now under the exclusive provisions of the Railway Act. There remain no substantial grounds today for preserving the separate treatment of certain transportation workers other than the fact that, being indisputably engaged in interstate commerce, they first came within the purview of federal legislation and so have long enjoyed special treatment. This distinction, like that between the law merchant and the law ecclesiastic, is now merely an historical curiosity.

In the preamble to the Constitution, written after our first experiment in independent government had demonstrated some patent weaknesses which we sought to correct, our founding fathers declared their purpose "to establish Justice, insure domestic Tranquillity . . . promote the general Welfare and secure the Blessings of Liberty to ourselves and our Posterity." It should be clear at this point that in the matter of industrial employment we have gotten quite far afield. We have disestablished justice; we have guaranteed constant controversy; we have promoted private privilege; and we have peddled the blessings of liberty for a mess of pottage. The money changers were thrown out of the temple in Jerusalem two thousand years ago. It is high time now to throw the pressure groups in Washington out of our legislative halls and out of our administrative agencies. We as a federal society have better things for our government to do than to grind the axes of these petty selfish interests. There are some very sound ideas presented there in the Constitution, both as to structure and procedure. We shall do well to reconsider them.

FOOTNOTES — V

[1] 29 U. S. Code Sec. 160, 161.

[2] See *The Struggle for Judicial Supremacy,* Robert H. Jackson, Alfred Knopf, New York, 1941, 106 *et seq.*

[3] See Archibald Cox, *Law and the National Labor Policy,* Institute of Industrial Relations, University of California, Berkeley, California, 1960, 52.

[4] Reference is made to the fixed rate of 52% on all net corporate income above $30,000 and to the low depreciation rates allowed such that acquisition of capital for expansion is seriously hampered for small concerns, and modernization discouraged in larger concerns.

[5] See Association of Westinghouse Salaried Employees v. Westinghouse Electric Corp., 75 S. Ct. 488, confirming 210 F. 2d 623 (1954).

[6] Erie Railroad v. Tompkins, 304 U. S. 64 (1938).

[7] 80 S. Ct. 1343, 1347, 1358, (1960) also see Paul R. Hays, "Supreme Court and Labor Law October Term 1959," 60 *Columbia Law Review* 901, 919-935 particularly.

[8] Paul R. Hays "Supreme Court & Labor Law, October Term 1959", 60 *Columbia Law Review,* 919-935.

[9] Professor E. H. Chamberlin of Harvard states: "The accumulated resources . . . for which union officers are now responsible directly or indirectly run into billions." "Labor Unions and Public Policy", *American Enterprise Association,* 1958, 2.

[10] For detailed discussion of separation of powers doctrine in Constitution see E. S. Corwin, editor, "The Constitution of the United States of America, Analysis and Interpretation," U. S. Government Printing Office, 1953, xvi *et seq.*

[11] *Ibid.,* xi *et seq.*

[12] *Constitution of the United States,* Amendments IX and X.

[13] 29 U. S. Code Sec. 164(c).

[14] Macmillan Company, New York.

[15] "The Labor Injunction", 210.

[16] *Ibid.,* see notes, 206.

[17] *Ibid.,* 203.

[18] See Railway Employees Dept., A.F.L. v. Hanson, 351 U. S. 225, 76 S. Ct. 714 (1956) and Gerard D. Reilly, "State Rights and the Law of Labor Relations," in *Labor Unions and Public Policy,* American Enterprise Association, Washington, 1958, 93-120.

[19] See I. Herbert Rothenberg, "National Emergency Disputes," *Labor Law Journal,* February, 1961, 108-146.

[20] 48 *Congressional Record* 6436, (1912).

[21] Williams v. Davis, 188 F. Supp. 916 and 81 S. Ct. 260 (1960).

[22] See *op. cit. The Labor Injunction,* Appendix I.

[23] See Table 6, Appendix A, 24th Annual Report National Labor Relations Board for Fiscal Year ended 30 June, 1959.

[24] 29 U. S. Code Sec. 160.

[25] 45 U. S. Code Sec. 153, 154.

[26] Letter of Senator McClellan on p. 108, *Labor Law Journal* (February 1961), is typical of a large number which were addressed to authorities in this field.

[27] 29 U. S. Code, Sec. 141-149.

[28] 45 U. S. Code Sec. 153.

[29] Eugene V. Rostow, *Planning for Freedom*, Yale University Press, 1959, 311.

[30] 11 U. S. Code, Sec. 11, 62.

[31] Paul R. Hays, *op. cit.*,

[32] 7 USC 182; 9 USC 1; 15 USC 12, 14, 44, 68, 1127; 18 USC 1951; 29 USC 142, 152, 176, 178, 203; 30 USC 4 (o); 33 USC 541; 45 USC 151.

[33] One of the chief strategies of the labor cartel to entrench itself is to make it unprofitable to move industry to low cost areas. The accelerated minimum wage is one technique and the industry-wide bargaining is another, both ingeniously rigged to keep the unemployed unemployed and to prevent capitalizing on geographic variations in unionization.

[34] As to Sweden, see address of Thorbjorn Carlsson, "A Look at Labor Management Relations in the Light of Swedish Experience", to Boston Chamber of Commerce, 11 October 1960; as to Switzerland, see "Labor Relations in Switzerland," *The Swiss Observer*, 25 March 1960.

[35] See Rexford G. Tugwell, *The Democratic Roosevelt*, Doubleday, Doran and Company, 1957, Chap. 19, and R. B. Morris, *Encyclopedia of American History*, Harper & Brothers, New York, 1953, 335 *et seq.*

[36] Hammer v. Dagenhart, 247 U. S. 251, (1918). Schechter Poultry Co. v. U. S., 295 U. S. 240, (1935).

[37] See 328 U. S. 108 (1945) and 156 2d 689 (1946); Farmers Reservoir and Irrigation Co. v. McComb, 337 U. S. 755 (1948); Lorain Journal Co. v. United States, 342 U. S. 222 (1951); and Southern United Ice Co. v. Hendrix, 153 F 2d 689 (1946).

[38] For comparable statement of congressional policy see 15 U. S. Code Sec. 1021.

[39] 45 U. S. Code Sec. 51-60.

[40] 46 U. S. Code Sec. 688.

[41] 33 U. S. Code Sec. 901 *et seq.*

[42] 42 U. S. Code Sec. 503.

[43] This is presently the standard established where an injured worker seeks compensation for his injury where it has occurred in "commerce", on the seas or railroads.

VI.
SUMMARY AND CONCLUSION

At the depth of the Great Depression a pattern of special privilege and immunity was established for union activities, and a special administrative agency was commissioned to enforce the pattern in order to create and maintain what was conceived to be a proper balance among the influences controlling the national economy. After a quarter century of experimentation and modification it is clear that there is a patent fallacy in the concept of achieving economic balance by putting a political foot on the union side of the scales of justice. This has encouraged an inflationary spiral and has entrenched its beneficiaries, but it has not proven a satisfactory formula for achievement of either full employment or industrial peace.

Not only have these ends had to be pursued primarily by other means but the whole perspective of our economic situation has altered so radically in the interim that much of the extraordinary political gimmickry we adopted a generation ago has become more an obstruction than an aid in handling the tremendous competitive assignment which has fallen our task in the world economic complex. Our national economy is not an isolated stage upon which puppets may be made to dance at will. Unions have been equipped to set wages in a vital sector of the economy as high as the traffic will bear, but the resultant price structure cannot long withstand the law of supply and demand. A host of economic ills follows in the wake of monopolistically controlled wages, quite as inexorably as in the wake of monopolistically controlled commodities. The true governor of the international economy is the consumers' sovereignty of which von Mises wrote.

Our whole creative energy needs to be released from these economic fetters to meet an unprecedented challenge just as the burgeoning nation-states of Europe needed two hundred years ago to be released from the fetters of Mercantilism. The tasks ahead demand from our social order the best ingenuity, the optimum individual incentives, and the strongest encouragement of those who are capable of increasing the diversity and adaptability, as well as the productivity, of our economy. Arbitrary restriction of competition anywhere tends to stultify ambition and resourcefulness. Special privilege on a vast scale breeds coercion and serious imbalance in our economy. It detracts ominously from the vitality of our whole society. This is the core of the problem of union power.

The growth of our society inevitably depends upon the cumulative cooperative efforts of its members. The cooperative effort which each citizen *sui juris* will exert and contribute clearly will vary with the incentive and inspiration offered him. The productivity of his effort will depend not merely on the worker's innate capacity and training or education but in even greater part upon the efficiency of the facilities afforded him and the competence of the management directing each enterprise. A congenial climate at the bar of justice is equally essential to the man whose income is derived directly from his labor, to the investor who risks his capital to furnish competitive facilities, to the managers responsible on the one hand for coordinating the use of labor, materials, and facilities, and on the other for balancing the income of sales with the expense of operation, and finally, to the members of the host community upon whom the logistics of the whole enterprise must depend.

Our illogical, self-contradictory, and prejudiced pattern of labor laws, designed in another economic era and burdened down by a depression-born preoccupation with the issue of initial recognition of the collective bargaining principle, have now for more than a generation denied to all these primary participants in our economic complex a proper access to common law justice in tort and contract. It betrays an appalling lack of confidence in our whole judicial system to presume it incompetent to comprehend or to handle the controversies arising in the daily relationships among workers and employers; yet this is exactly the presumption upon which our whole massive complex of federal labor statutes and regulations has been predicated.

The fundamental philosophy of our whole system of government, the very fountainhead of Anglo-American jurisprudence, lies embodied in the concept that our communities are capable of self-government, but by the pernicious authoritarian doctrine of federal pre-emption we have persistently and increasingly encroached upon the prerogatives of self-government in our component states until today they are denied many of the most elementary aspects of jurisdiction in the field of industrial relations. And while our constitutionally balanced local governmental bodies have been precluded from exercising even the powers of self-defense in these matters, the power of national economic strangulation, without a single effective check or balance short of martial law, has been permitted to pass by default to a small group of privileged intermediaries whose methods, objectives, and ambitions are totally beyond the reach of our basic constitutional safeguards. It is indeed a situation which appears to belie Lincoln's aphorism that you can't fool all the people all the time. International monopolies in the field of employment are no more essential to our national well-being than are cartels controlling commodities.

Mr. Jefferson declared that periodic revolutions spaced about a generation apart would be a healthy thing. He meant that there is a tendency in men's affairs for power to gravitate into certain institutions that live substantially beyond the life span of the individual and that each generation should undertake to reconsider and determine for itself those vital decisions made by default or deliberation before those upon whom the burdens were imposed had acquired the capacity of adulthood. There is certainly adequate provocation in the United States today for some revolutionary redrafting of our very peculiar system for dispensing justice in the economic field.

The fundamental rights of millions of innocent bystanders have been virtually ignored in the power struggle between behemoth corporations and behemoth labor unions. Too long have we forgotten in our economic planning the cardinal maxims of constitutional government—the separation of powers, the equality of privileges, and the limited authority of federal bureaucracy. The time has come for us to restore to the judiciary the full scope of judicial function, to revive in our component States an awareness of their responsibility for local economic conditions, and to persistently acknowledge the prerogatives of self-government among our communities in the economic field. Standardization and centralization have been overly convenient devices whereby those with hunger for power could distort the national economy and the federal budget.

We must discard the mad illusion that we can successfully maintain a competitive economy while nurturing throughout our industrial complex the most virulent kind of monopoly over manpower. The special immunities and privileges of the bosses of national and international labor unions must be stricken from the statute books along with the hereditary privileges of the landed aristocracy and feudal lords. The preposterously top-heavy superstructure of federal bureaucracy, created by hopeful fence-straddlers whose answer to every problem has been the establishment of another special commission or bureau to conduct studies or implement the requests of special interests, must be shaken down to permit primary attention to be directed at the essentials, those matters of truly national significance, e.g. national defense, foreign policy, the administration of justice, the regulation of monopolies, and the construction of such vital public works as cannot otherwise be managed.

The first step in the restoration of constitutional procedures in the economic life of our federal republic is the modification of the Norris-LaGuardia Act so as to put the union hierarchy back on the same footing with other citizens in the field of equity jurisdiction and to restore full cognizance of employment contracts and torts to the judicial arm of government. Not since the vindictive monstrosities of the Reconstruction Era were perpetrated upon the South has such a distortion of fundamental justice prevailed in our federal system. Next the National

Labor Relations Act should be amended to rescind the assignment of judicial functions to an administrative department which has ample burdens without the task of operating a secondary system of ersatz courts. The judiciary should then be reinforced to handle the tens of thousands of controversies which now arise annually in interpretation of the substantive provisions of the employment statutes. The access to State courts should be opened wide, as in the case of the Federal Employers Liability Act, and the scope of federal jurisdiction reduced, by proper definition of the word "commerce", to its true constitutional dimensions. Finally, as an interim measure, every third-party whose legitimate access to his own livelihood has been unreasonably damaged, interfered with, or cut off by the economic warfare tactics of employers or union leaders should be given a cause of action in federal court for proper remedy. Certainly the sacred cow of "concerted action" belongs as much to 100,000 stranded commuters as to 62 displaced tugboat crewmen. If the first are denied the use of public transportation not involved in any dispute, surely the latter have no vested interest in the former's inconvenience.

The reconstruction era for national economy after the Great Depression produced as much ill-considered legislation as did the Reconstruction Era after the War Between the States. The time has come to re-examine with a clear head the whole peculiar rationale of our existing statutes in the field of industrial relations. We well may find that a fair revision of those laws, reforming them to our constitutional principles, will generate by its example alone the greatest economic bonanza since the overthrow of Mercantilism two hundred years ago.